Preliminary exercises

Comprehensions

General exercises

Exercise One – Signal words

1   Technique ('How does the author' suggests focus on language).

2   Technique (signal word: 'vivid'). You are asked to focus on techniques the author uses to bring the market to life.

3   Recall (signal words: 'In your own words'). You only have to retrieve from the text.

4   Response. Your engagement with the text is the focus of the question, not what can be inferred from it.

5   Thought. The question is about character.

6   Recall. Despite the signal words 'How does the author' the question then does not focus on how the text is written but on what it is saying, on the content. You only have to retrieve the answer from the text.

7   Response. Your reaction to the text is what the question asks about.

8   Technique (signal words: 'How does the author' and 'vivid'). The question is asking about the effectiveness of language.

9   Thought (signal words: 'What impression'). The question is asking for inference of character.

10 Thought (signal word: 'think). You are being asked to give an answer based on the text and the clues in it.

Exercise Two – How to answer

1   Recall question. 1 mark for the answer (only one point to make).

2   Thought (think) question, as you have to infer from the text. 3 PEELs (2 marks per PEEL).

3   Thought question, as you have to infer character from the text. 3 PEELs (2 marks per PEEL).

4   Technique question ('How does the author'). 3 PEELs (2 marks per PEEL).

5   Thought or response question, depending on how closely you have to work with the text; usually it will be thought. 3 PEELs, even though only 5 marks. If response, then write as well as you can – there is no strict allocation of marks.

6   As Q5.

7   Recall question. 1 mark per point, so make two points.

8   Technique question (about effectiveness of language). 2 PEELs (2 marks per PEEL).

9   Technique question (about effectiveness of language). 2 PEELs (2 marks per PEEL).

10 Response. Write as well as you can – there is no strict allocation of marks.

Exercise Three – Recall practice

Note: answers should be in sentences.

1 Queen, worker and drone. (1 mark per type mentioned).

2 Through scent markers (but must be in own words, e.g. through pheromones).

3 No one (or not queen). All bees together decide. (1 mark per point made).

4 Any two of the following (or similar, but own words): bringing up the larvae, removing dirt from the hive, making sure no intruders come into the hive, foraging.

5 Exhaustion.

6 They die.

Exercise Four – Explaining imagery

1 A bulldog is a short, stocky dog with a slightly squashed face and hanging cheeks, which is quite aggressive. Here, the simile suggests that the teacher's face is blunt and flat and that her cheeks are sagging, probably due to age. The simile also carries the connotation that the teacher is not necessarily friendly, but possibly quite aggressive.

2 Clockwork is a mechanical form of energy that depends on a spring unwinding and cogs falling into place. The movements produced by clockwork are usually quite hacked-off. The simile suggests the blackbirds keep moving independently, but in a cut-off, jerky way that suggests they are not being powered by muscles.

3 A spider's web is made of sticky strands that capture insects. When an insect, like a fly, hits the web, it is stuck and though it struggles it is usually caught, enabling the spider to paralyse and eat it. Here, the simile suggests the person quivering is helpless and moving frantically in a vain attempt to break free from an imminent, dangerous situation.

4 A kettle drum is a big, deep drum that has loud and long beats. The simile suggests that the heart is booming loudly and sonorously, mirroring the fear the person is feeling. This is underlined by the vacuum of fear. Although sound would not travel in a vacuum, the idea here is that the heart is all alone and thus even more scared.

5 A police car on the prowl moves slowly, trying to take in everything, because it is looking for something, or some crime, to pick up on. The movements of the car are smooth and deliberate, ready to either stop or accelerate. Here the simile suggests the bird is moving easily through the sky, but looking left and right, ready for anything to happen. The simile suggests that the bird might be looking for trouble or sees itself as someone called to keep order.

Exercise Five – Sound effects

1 Crunched: The hard initial 'cr' sound is reminiscent of breaking through a hard surface, though not with too much force, which mirrors the foot going through the hard topmost layer of snow. The following 'ch' sound is softer and wetter, like packing something slightly slushier together, which is what happens in the lower layer of snow, when the foot hits the ground underneath.

2 Struck: The initial 'st' sound is hard and forceful; the plosive 't' suggests a short and sharp hit, which is underlined by the hard 'ck' sound at the end, which again sounds like a sharp impact.

3 The alliteration of the hard 'g' sound suggests something difficult to move, which is strengthened by the addition of the low, rumbling 'r', in 'ground', which seems to catch on the initial 'g' sound. The whole impression is of something rusty or heavy slowly starting to move or coming to a halt.

4 Jingled: The 'jin' sound is short and light, which mirrors the sound of little bells. While the 'j' suggests some form of percussion, the sound is soft enough to be pleasant and in combination with the 'i' seems to be more a light touch than a real hit.

5 The alliterated 'b' sound is quite round and open, although percussive, so is more of a large, probably softer surface impacting on another than a hit or stab The repetition of this sound suggests that the car is repeatedly impacting on the road, with multiple softer, drawn-out percussions. The 'p', which is similar enough to the 'b', is a sudden, harder hit, suggesting something like a potholed road with many minor holes and one bigger one.

Exercise Six – Common techniques

1 The use of the first person pronoun here suggests that the speaker is in a team with the audience and they are both in the problem together. It serves to motivate the audience by suggesting all are working together.

2 The rhetorical question does not need an answer, as it is obvious that no matter whom you ask, everybody wants to be happy. The question is being used to prepare the ground, as the audience will believe that whatever comes after the question will help to make them happy.

3 The list here emphasises how much the sister bought. This effect is reinforced by the fact she does not only buy one of everything, but more. The close succession of different items she bought suggests there are many more, that the whole shopping is an unmanageable pile.

4 This repetition of the same phrase at the beginning of different clauses reinforces the idea that all that is being thought is probably wrong, as the 'may' suggests a contrast coming. The repetition hammers home the message as it builds up a certain rhythm that is almost inescapable.

5 The tense change here brings the tapping on Peter's shoulder to the present. As such it interrupts the flow of the story that was comfortably in the past tense and makes the happening immediate, as the tense shift suggests it is happening now, at the moment the reader reads the words.

6 Hyperbole is being used here to persuade people to recycle. The consequences of not recycling are exaggerated in an emotional way, pretending that the world will regress enormously. This is not true, of course, but the exaggeration, paired with the inherent emotional appeal, is hard to avoid, as we react strongly to shocking news.

7 The rhyming couplet at the end makes the last two lines flow more and links them. Due to the rhyme the last line seems a natural follow-on from the line before, making it more inevitable and forceful. The fact that the words have lost their light leads automatically to the poet no longer writing a love-song.

8 The two commands are a direct and forceful way of saying things. The terseness of them also seems to solicit an immediate response, making the addressee start writing. The effect is to shake the addressee up with abruptness to make her or him do what is being said.

9 The short sentence comes after a series of longer sentences, which describe Hal's run down the pitch. The sentences are long, mirroring his running and winning streak. The punctuation of the clauses follows his movements. However, when he slips and is abruptly brought to a halt, the syntax mirrors this, too, as the sentence is short, breaking the flow, much like the slip breaks the flow of the running.

10 The capital letters here emphasise the word 'that'. The capitals could mean that the speaker is shouting the words, but it could also be that she merely wants to emphasise them. The emphasis shows she is shocked at what has been done to her. The fact that she does not even name the deed shows her shock as well as the capitals; the deed seems too bad to mention.

Exercise Seven – Inferring character

1   merciful: although the opposing Cimbri have killed many Romans and it would be usual in war to at least lock up the prisoners, Caesar releases them to return home. This shows that Caesar takes pity on the captives that are in his power, meaning he is merciful.

2   jealous: although her boyfriend is only laughing with someone else, Isabel already feels she needs to do something to make the girl look bad. She is obviously not happy to see her boyfriend talk to another girl, as she is suspicious he might prefer the other girl. So she spills her drink over the girl, showing her jealousy.

3   impulsive: Jeff had not planned on buying ice cream: he only wanted milk. On seeing it, he acts on the spur of the moment as he suddenly wants the ice cream. This is impulsive: acting without forethought.

4   honest: given the fact that the question was not clear, Caspar could obviously have hidden his involvement in the affair or even pretended not to understand. Instead he says everything, showing he is honest, as he does not hide anything.

5   forgiving: although Holly was mean to Alice, when Holly is subsequently in distress, Alice is prepared to forget that Holly hurt her and tries to comfort her. This shows that she is forgiving as she stops feeling angry towards Holly and only reacts to her need for support.

6   scheming: James knows that he has little chance of becoming prefect, so he acts unfairly to try and reach his goal. He acts in secret, without other people knowing what he is doing and uses underhand methods to try and become prefect, showing he is scheming.

7   thoughtful: although the other pupils react instantly and noisily to the news that they have to re-do prep, Eva does not join in, but looks carefully at her work and thinks about her mistakes and whether it is fair to ask her to re-do it. By not acting immediately, but reflecting on the matter, Eva shows herself to be thoughtful.

8   dreamy: David is watching a sporting event, which would usually capture the focus of a boy. He stares at the sky, though, and uses his imagination to colour his observation. This shows he is dreamy, as he lets his mind slip to other things than what he is meant to be concentrating on.

Exercise Eight – Stairway to heaven

For some words other usages exist: I have only used the most common here. Sentences that illustrate the meaning are for example purposes only.

1   fast
   (a)   He ran so fast that no-one else could keep up with him.
   (b)   The hook held fast to the wall and could not be removed.
   (c)   In Lent most Christians fast for some time, only eating one small meal a day.
   (d)   I was at the station too early because my watch was fast.

2   apt
   (a)   Because he is apt to run away when faced with danger, they held on to him tightly.
   (b)   'Lightning Jones' was an apt name for him, as he finished all work before anyone else.

3   bow
   (a)   He put on his dinner jacket and a black bow tie.
   (b)   She nocked an arrow to the string and raised the bow menacingly.
   (c)   The bow of the ship cut through the waves as she sped westwards.
   (d)   When the Chinese emperor arrived, the servant bowed low to the ground.

(e) The president could see no other alternative but to bow to the pressure of the unions and give them what they wanted.

(f) She picked up the violin and drew the bow over its strings, making it scream like a tortured cat.

4 pole

(a) The North Pole is not the same as the magnetic North Pole.

(b) A red and white striped pole outside a shop used to show it was a barber's shop.

(c) Although we usually agree, in questions of fashion Jake and I are poles apart.

5 bear

(a) She was so exhausted, she couldn't bear to run another mile.

(b) The grizzly bear caught the salmon in mid-jump.

(c) In hot countries donkeys bear most loads.

(d) The apple tree will bear lots of fruits this year.

(e) When you get to the crossing, bear right.

6 follow

(a) The children followed the teacher out onto the lawn, making sure no one overtook her.

(b) From what you said it does not follow that he is guilty, as there are other explanations for his behaviour.

(c) They followed the tennis match with great interest as they hoped the German would lose.

7 bark

(a) To reach the galleon they had to take a bark.

(b) The bark of the oak was knobbly and ridged, showing its age much like wrinkles.

(c) The dog was so excited it didn't stop barking.

(d) The general barked out orders on the parade ground.

8 change

(a) I paid with a ten pound note and put the £7.51 change I received in my pocket.

(b) Don't look while I'm changing into my sports kit.

(c) If you do not change the way you approach Latin sentences you will never translate them correctly.

9 order

(a) 'Are you ready to order?' the waiter asked.

(b) The captain ordered the soldiers to attack.

(c) You must answer these questions in the right order, starting at number one.

(d) The judge called for order in the courtroom, as the audience was noisy.

(e) She wrote poetry of the highest order and justly received many awards for it.

10 trunk

(a) She put all her clothes in a big leather trunk, as her bag was too small.

(b) He walked to the pool in his brand new swimming trunks.

(c) As the man had told him, after 300 yards he came to a trunk road where he had to give way to crossing traffic.

(d) The keeper tickled the elephant's trunk.

(e) The tree was old and had a thick trunk from which a number of stout branches sprouted.

11 row

(a) The choir was told to line up in three rows with the tallest at the back.

(b) At the boat races this year Cambridge rowed its way to victory.

(c) John and Jack could never agree on anything and now they were having a row about which cereal was better.

Exercises for Poetry Comprehensions

Exercise Nine – Get rhythm

The stressed syllables are in capitals.

1 If E–ver i LAY my HANDS on the BRA–zen BUR–glar

2 The RA–ttlesnake HISSED MER–ci–LESS–ly at the FRIGH–tened SQUIRREL.
or
The RA–ttle–SNAKE hissed MER–ci–LESS–ly AT the FRIGH–tened SQUIRREL. (iambic heptameter)

3 The WI–zard KNEW his TIME had COME. (iambic tetrameter)

4 FLU–ffy LI–ttle BU–nnies RUN–ning MAD–ly (trochaic pentameter)

5 If the WAVE hits the BOAT we will DROWN in the SWELL. (anapaestic tetrameter)

6 The CAP–tain WAS a–FRAID of CRO–co–DILES. (iambic pentameter)

7 Noc–TUR–nal CREA–tures OF–ten USE their HEAR–ing to FIND their PREY.

Exercise Ten – Rhyme time

1 full rhyme

2 rhyme scheme is AABBA (the poem is a limerick)

3 half rhyme

4 consonant rhyme

5 cross rhyme (lines 1 & 3 and 2 & 4 rhyme); lines 2 & 4 are, strictly speaking, a half rhyme

6 rhyming couplet (with a full rhyme)

Writing tasks

The answers in this section are suggestions only: there are many correct ways to answer the questions. Note: where sentences have been corrected, this does not mean they are necessarily stylistically good.

General exercises

Exercise One – Making sense of sentences

These are suggestions only: there are many ways to correct these. Note: just because the sentences have been corrected does not mean they are necessarily stylistically good.

1 Humming a tune to himself, he walked through the cityscape, watching the people stream by.

2 He had cornered the enemy, who was ready to kill him, and drew his gun, knowing that this might be the end.

3 He pressed him to the floor as he lost consciousness.

4 The gloomy light seeped through the window.

5 He looked at the trees tapping against the window and swaying madly in the wind, thinking why was he there.

6 I ran through the heather so bright and purple, which was stretched out to the horizon as far as I could see.

7 Because he was busy he didn't see the men, thinking he was safe in the home with the alarm protecting him.

Exercise Two – Making sure there were no there were

1 A crowd of people demonstrated in the city.

2 Many books lay scattered around on the library tables.

3 Many cows paced thoughtfully through the field.

4 A slight problem made itself noticeable.

5 This prison has no way out.

Exercise Three – Tightening prose

Boughs tugged at my shirt as I ran scared through the woods towards a distant home. The forest was pitch black. As I ran, blindly, branches whipped across my arms and face, stinging them like wires of heat. Although disorientated, I kept to one direction, hoping it would lead me out. Suddenly I stumbled on a root that had snaked onto the path. I went flying and my ankle twisted beneath me. I screamed in pain. I was no longer able to run.

Prose for a purpose

Exercise Four – Beginnings

The following are examples of each type of introduction.

1 Own experience
Each term ends the same way: from half term to the dreaded exam week, all pupils are in a frenzy of revision, nerves and insufficient sleep. Apart from the exams there are manifold tests, be they spelling or French vocab, strewn throughout the year. In fact, in my experience, never a week goes by in which there is not some form of examination.

2 Current affairs/historical link
If the education secretary is to be believed, then A-levels will change again very soon. After what he calls a 'dumbing-down' of these exams, he advocates a stricter approach to ensure only top pupils really achieve a top grade. But why all these tests? Aren't British pupils tested enough?

3 Definition of the tittle
For the purposes of this discussion I will take exams to mean any form of test that the pupils have to complete in the course of ordinary school time and which is not necessary to gain access to any other school or course. More contentious, and of greater interest, is the question of what precisely 'too many' means. This will form the main point of my discussion.

4 Proverb or saying
'The proof of the pudding is in the eating' suggests that the best test is to see whether something does what it is intended to do, rather than to laboriously devise experiments. Similarly, one could argue that artificial tests of knowledge, such as exams, are no test for whether pupils have learnt or are more educated.

5 Cultural link
In mythology, the sphinx devoured travellers who were unable to answer her riddle. Though exams are not quite as opaque as the sphinx's riddle and the consequences of failing them are not quite as dire, they nevertheless hold a thrall over education similar to that of the sphinx over Thebes, scaring away people and making them want to avoid them.

6 Repeat title in own words

Children going to school in the United Kingdom are tested far too much in the course of any academic year.

Exercise Five – The end

Once again these are suggestions only.

How do you spend your holiday?

When you look at it analytically, the holidays don't sound too exciting and it seems that I do more or less the same thing every day: playing (either alone or with friends) and going on little trips. Even the differences between going somewhere else for a holiday and staying at home is not that large. However, what makes holidays different and worthwhile is that what I do on any given day is largely my decision. This element of choice breaks up the monotony and makes the holidays what they are meant to be: a little time of freedom in an otherwise busy year filled with school work.

A good book will always make you think

Not all good books are written to make you think. But even those that are meant to make you laugh will have something to engage the intellect, like well-written dialogue that challenges the brain's versatility. Mostly, though, books in which we care for the main characters will make us think, especially when the characters are faced with difficulties or are treated unfairly. At such moments we empathise with the characters and think what we would do. By living vicariously through them we learn how to possibly deal with such situations, meaning a good book will not only make us think, but actually let us learn important lessons for life.

Creative writing

Exercise Six – A different spin

These are some suggestions.

1 A Day in the Sun

Could be literal: a day in the core of the sun – as a scientist or probe; writing as a lizard or snake in the desert and about basking; a day when everything went right and you were metaphorically in the sun.

2 Behind the Door

The variety with this title will stem less from what the door could be than what might be behind any form of aperture. Could be underground tunnel system, a secret room (think Bluebeard), a new school or another door or a labyrinth. Metaphorically, it could be going through to a new phase of life. Also, think of switched pov, so this could be about a trapdoor spider or a trapdoor spider's almost prey.

3 My Favourite Teacher

Could be vocational teacher; could be from young animal's pov and teacher is mother; could be about famous person who is a teacher (but not yours); failure could be favourite teacher and story thus about time when you failed and what it taught you; could be a certain place you go to think; could be books!

4 The Waiting-Room

As with the door, the variety will depend on the type of room more than on giving the title itself a different spin. Think prison cell as room to either death or release, womb (waiting to be born), coffin (waiting to be resurrected), antechamber for the last judgement, outside the headmaster's study, car as waiting room on wheels. Could switch to pov of the room itself. You could interpret the title to mean a room that is waiting for something. This could be food (the room being a trap – could change to pov of beetle or similar), decorations (e.g. room waiting for Christmas decorations) or someone to arrive (e.g. palace waiting for new monarch).

5 Break

This could be a pause of any kind in any kind of activity: so not only in school or in an office, but a break in fighting or a break in a conversation. Break could be short for a break-in or break-out. Break could also be two people splitting up, a piece of earth falling off from a larger mass, an opening of the ground or waves breaking as they come to the shore.

Exercise Seven – Different beginnings

These are examples. Many others are possible.

The Disused Station

1 Dialogue

'The door isn't locked; we can go in,' Martin exclaimed as he turned the matted brass handle of the paint-stripped door.

Elizabeth held back, not sure whether she should join her brother. After all, the old station house did not look stable: the ridge of the roof was broken and the missing tiles looked like badly patched wounds.

2 Onomatopoeia

Da-dunk, da-dunk – da-dunk, da-dunk

Tom could hear the rattle of steel wheels on rails, the pumping of the pistons, the soft hiss of steam and the quiet, almost peaceful bubbling of the water in the tank of an engine pulling up into the station. Only there was no train.

3 Setting

At the end of the valley, where it bends out of sight as though ashamed of its sudden halt at a cliff face, overshadowed by the boulders of the mountains and huddling against them for comfort, stood the faded remains of the station house. It had never been important or attractive and had only gained a certain grace and dignity now, in its decay.

4 Mystery

Jim couldn't explain it. And yet he wasn't entirely sure it was anything worth explaining. But whenever he pressed the tune button up from 105.4 FM, searching for the next station, the radio always and inexplicably stopped at 106.1, although there was no broadcast. It was spooky. So spooky he had to try it again and again and showed his friends, too.

Exercise Eight – Extending similes

These are examples only.

1 Leaves swirled in the air like bits of paper that had fallen out of a person's diary and in their faded, creased shapes held the remains of someone's life in their curled hands.

2 In his anger he shouted as loudly as a thunderstorm that had built and boiled slowly over a mountain range to come crashing down with purple lightning in one great onslaught.

3 The rose was as red as blood that moved slowly and darkly in a heart hurt too many times.

4 The clouds rushed across the sky like sailing boats with sails billowing, their hulls silver streaks on a shimmering sea.

5 She stood as still as a statue that had been carved centuries ago and was now pockmarked and corroded by time, its limbs broken off and the joints crumbling.

6 The thief moved as stealthily as a mouse that had lost its family to a cat and wanted to show its prowess by stealing some of its dry food from directly under its nose.

2 Literary prose comprehensions

Shadow of the Past

LEVEL 2

Question	Type and structure	Answer possibilities
1 Three things that haven't changed in the classroom	**Recall** 3 marks – 1 mark per point made	• chalkboards flaked • chalkboards in need of repair • chalk is there • only little stubs of chalk there • view out of the window (of mountains)
2 How does the author make uni seem uncanny (lines 1–9)?	**Technique** 4 marks – 2 PEELs Per PEEL, 1 mark for point and evidence, 1 mark for explanation	• short statement: 'Not many people seem to be around' – short sentence drives home message that no-one is around. A uni should be bustling, that it is not seems strange (only later does he realise why the uni is deserted). • describing detail: 'Huge and strange gables' – gables are the top part of a building. If this is large and unusual, then it is like something weird is looming over the building, shadowing it and creating a sense of tension or fear. • describing detail: 'old dark-brown brick' – old edifices tend to be more atmospheric; that the brick is dark-brown reminds of old sepia photographs, suggesting the uni comes from another century, which could be slightly spooky. • use of dialogue: 'Why are we going inside?' – if Chris questions the decision to go inside then there must be good reasons not to go inside. Chris's fear is transferred to the reader, making the uni uncanny. • onomatopoeia: 'creak' – slight crunching 'kr' sound mirrors the step on the floor and the 'eek' the response of the wood, like a quiet scream. Creaking floorboards are scary because they suggest a building that can hear the approach of someone in an otherwise silent environment. • short sentences: 'Halfway up I stop and listen. There's no sound at all.' – a completely silent atmosphere is oppressive as there should be some sounds of life. No sound suggests death, which is uncanny in a building. The short sentences underline the silence as they do not break it for long and are almost hushed in their brevity.

Question	Type and structure	Answer possibilities
3 How does the author bring across the strangeness of being where he used to be as someone else?	**Technique** 6 marks – 3 PEELs Per PEEL, 1 mark for point and evidence, 1 mark for explanation	• use of third person singular: 'he' – although he is talking about himself, he uses the third person singular, as though it wasn't him, but someone else who was there, which is strange. • italics: 'Of *him*?' – the fact that the author is listening for sounds of his former self is strange, as he is that same person. The italics emphasise that he feels he is someone else, which is strange. • metaphor: 'I am the ghost' – although the author is there, the fact that he feels like a ghost, an unreal, ephemeral being that has no physicality, suggests that he is haunting a place where he should not be. • personal pronoun: 'I see his hand' – he is describing his own hand as belonging to someone else, leading to a sense of disjointedness. • short sentence: 'He is here now' – the fact that the author says there is someone there, although there isn't, makes the scene uncanny. The short sentence and the italics emphasise the strangeness of the double presence. • metaphor: 'everything jumps forth and vibrates with recall' – the surroundings seem to loom in on him and ripple around him as he moves through what must be memories and reality merging. It is like being beside oneself and reality does not seem stable, adding to the sense of strangeness.
4 What do we learn about the author?	**Thought** 6 marks – 3 PEELs Per PEEL, 1 mark for point and evidence, 1 mark for explanation	• focused: 'I just shake my head' – he is trying to get into the atmosphere of the place and Chris is disrupting him. He does not answer as he is intent on what he is doing, so only gestures. • determined: 'I'm staying' – although Chris is obviously distressed, Pirsig is determined to carry on and find out what he can; less determined people would stop their quest to look to Chris. • lets people be independent/uncaring: 'Go outside then' – instead of comforting his son, as most fathers would, he lets him go his own way/tells him to leave. • meditative: 'stare out the window at the mountains' – while his pupils work, he looks at the distance, obviously thinking about things, as he does not seem to be daydreaming. The later mention of 'oneness' suggests he finds some form of calm like in meditation. • dedicated: 'He gave everything to it' – this means that he put all of himself into his teaching, so more than was necessary. He did not see it as a job you do and then stop to go home, which suggests he is dedicated.

Question	Type and structure	Answer possibilities
5 In which way was his classroom 'a thousand rooms'?	**Thought** 6 marks – 3 PEELs Per PEEL, 1 mark for point and evidence, 1 mark for explanation	• physical change outside affects the room: 'changing … with the storms and snows and patterns of clouds' – for him the scenery outside is part of the room, and part of meditations in it and this changes on a daily basis, making the room never the same room twice. • group dynamics shape the room: 'with each class' – the room is more than just the walls; the people in it define the room as well. Depending on which class he had in the room, the room changed, as the people inside it changed and the way they dealt with each other was different each time. • each individual puts their mark on the room: 'even with each student' – every single person in the room made it a different room. If on one day one student were absent, the room would be different for lack of that student. But as each student is different each day (moods change, thoughts develop), the room becomes different each time. • Time changes the room, too: 'No two hours were ever alike' – as things change with time, so the room would change too. Viewed as a whole made up of space, the people in it and time, the room would change every second.

LEVEL 1

Question	Type and structure	Answer possibilities
1 What three things have not changed in the classroom?	**Recall** 3 marks – 1 mark per point made	• chalkboards flaked • chalkboards in need of repair • chalk is there • only little stubs of chalk there • view out of the window (of mountains)
2(a) Quotations that show how the author makes uni uncanny	**Technique (split)** **Evidence (2 marks)** 1 mark per appropriate quotation	• 'Not many people seem to be around' • 'Huge and strange gables' • 'old dark-brown brick' • 'Why are we going inside?' • 'creak' • 'Halfway up I stop and listen. There's no sound at all.'
2(b) Explain quotations	**Explanation (4 marks)** 2 marks per explanation; simple explanation will get 1 mark	(In same order as the quotations above.) • short sentence drives home message that no-one is around. A uni should be bustling, that it is not seems strange. • the gables are the top part of a building. If this is large and unusual, then it is like something weird is looming over the building, shadowing it and creating a sense of tension or fear. • old buildings tend to be more scary; that the brick is dark-brown reminds of old photographs, suggesting the uni comes from another century, which is spooky. • if Chris doesn't want to go inside then there must be good reasons not to. The reader feels Chris's fear, making the uni feel uncanny. • creaking floorboards are scary because they suggest a silent building that seems to be listening out for you. • a completely silent atmosphere is scary as there should be some sounds of life. No sounds at all suggest death, which is negative and spooky.
3(a) Quotations that show the strangeness of being where he used to teach but as a different person	**Technique (split)** **Evidence (2 marks)** 1 mark per appropriate quotation	• 'Of *him*?' • 'I am the ghost' • 'I see his hand' • 'He is here now' • 'Everything jumps forth and vibrates with recall'

Question	Type and structure	Answer possibilities
3(b) Explain how the effect is created	**Explanation (*4 marks*)** 2 marks per explanation; simple explanation will get 1 mark	(In same order as the quotations above.) • the fact that the author is listening for sounds of who he used to be is strange, as he is that same person. The italics emphasise that he feels he is someone else, which is not normal. • although the author is there, in reality, he feels like a ghost, an unreal spirit that haunts places where it should not be. This shows he feels out of place and unreal. • Pirsig is describing his own hand as belonging to someone else, leading to a sense of being someone different to who he is or was, which is strange. • the author says there is someone there, although there isn't, which makes the scene uncanny. The short sentence and the italics emphasise the strangeness of two people being where there is only one person. • the surroundings seem to bear down on him and ripple around him as he moves through the memories, which he is not sure are his own. It is like being beside and reality does not seem stable.
4 Impressions of the author	**Thought** 2 + 4 marks – 2 PEELs Per PEEL, 1 mark for point and evidence, 2 marks for explanation; simple explanation will get 1 mark	• determined: 'I'm staying' – although Chris is obviously distressed, Pirsig is determined to carry on and find out what he can; less determined people would stop their quest to look after Chris or reassure Chris before going on. • lets people be independent/uncaring: 'Go outside then' – instead of comforting his son, as most fathers would, he lets him go his own way/tells him to leave. This can be considered uncaring, but it also lets Chris go his own way. • meditative: 'stare out the window at the mountains' – while his pupils work, he looks at the distance, obviously thinking about things, as he does not seem to be daydreaming. It seems like he is trying to find some calm, as he later mentions a feeling of 'oneness'. • dedicated: 'He gave everything to it' – this means that he put all of himself into his teaching, so did not just see it as a job he stopped doing as soon as he went home. For him it was part of his life, part of himself.
5 What does the author mean by his classroom was 'a thousand rooms'?	**Thought** 4 marks – 2 PEELs Per PEEL, 1 mark for point and evidence, 1 mark for simple explanation	• physical change outside affects the room: 'changing … with the storms and snows and patterns of clouds' – for him the scenery outside is part of the room and as this changes, so does the room. • the people in the room make it different each time: 'with each class, and even with each student' – the room is more than just the walls; the people in it define the room as well. Depending on which class he had in the room, the room changed. • time changes the room, too: 'No two hours were ever alike' – as things change with time, so the room would change too. No two moments are ever the same and so the room changed the whole time, too.

LEVEL 2

Question	Type and structure	Answer possibilities
1 In own words the rules governing exercise in London	**Recall** 2 marks – 1 mark per point made Must be own words	• you can move rapidly to avert a mishap • you should not exercise or move rapidly for purposes of fitness
2 How does the author make the reaction humorous (lines 17–33)	**Technique** 6 marks – 3 PEELs Per PEEL, 1 mark for point and evidence, 1 mark for explanation	• itemised list: '(a) … (k)' – normally a list would show that there are many people watching, but by drawing up an itemised list, the author suggests that it is important to mention everyone looking on. The humour resides in length of list as well as contrast between solemnity of the list and the unimportance of the event it is being made for. • repetition: 'Hotel Mathis … Hotel Previtali' – it would be sufficient to list the people from the hotel, but by separating out both hotels and the various employees, it seems that the people come in groups and also that the hotels, competitors in business, are now also competitors in gawping, which is humorous. • hyperbole: 'even the cat' – the cat would not really be laughing, and the suggestion it does sounds ridiculous, leading to humour. It also reminds of cartoon cats laughing, which adds to the humour. • use of brackets: '(one intoxicated)' – the information in the brackets is unnecessary, but it adds humour as it suggests that it is the kind of spectacle a drunkard would enjoy. • use of numbers: 'eleven … twenty-seven' – the fact that one person doing exercise can draw such a crowd is humorous, as exaggerated. The contrast between the simple act of exercising and a huge crowd like one would expect at an accident or similar, is humorous. • rivalry between the hotels: 'four waiters … six waiters' – that both hotel staff watch is already humorous, as they stop all work to watch one man exercise. That the exact number of each type of employee is mentioned and juxtapositioned for each hotel, adds to the comic effect as the hotels seem to be trying to outdo each other at watching a man exercise.
3 How does Ashe make people accept his fitness regime?	**Recall** 4 marks – 1 mark per point made	• through patience • through perseverance • by not letting himself be put off by the laughter • by continuing to do his exercises regularly for a month, by which time only children watch • by keeping on doing the exercises for three months, when they are accepted

Question	Type and structure	Answer possibilities
4 What kind of a person is Ashe?	**Thought** 6 marks – 3 PEELs Per PEEL, 1 mark for point and evidence, 1 mark for explanation	• confident: 'whirled his Indian clubs' – although London frowns on exercise, he goes out onto the street to keep fit, showing he is confident enough to face ridicule. • determined: 'a month later' – although he was scorned for exercising, he does not give up and keeps exercising until the neighbours accept him. • smartly dressed and well-off: 'sweater, flannel trousers' – although shorts would not have been wide-spread for exercise in those days, he sounds smartly dressed, as flannel trousers are finer material, suggesting he takes care of his appearance and is quite well-off. • believes in healing power of exercise: 'wished to expel by means of physical fatigue a small devil of discontent' – he is troubled in his mind and resorts to exercise to try and calm him, which shows he believes fitness is the answer to most problems. • focused: 'measured and solemn fashion' – he breathes out slowly and seriously before starting his exercises, which shows that he is focused, getting into 'exercise mode' where nothing will disturb him.
5(a) Why does Ashe do Larsen Exercises	**Recall** 1 mark – 1 mark for appropriate point	• to expel ... a small devil of discontent
5(b) What kind of exercises are they?	**Thought** 6 marks – 3 PEELs Per PEEL, 1 mark for point and evidence, 1 mark for explanation	• the apex of fitness: 'the last word in exercises' – if something is the last word, then it is the latest and best, suggesting the Larsen Exercises are the best type of fitness regime there is. • involve the whole body: 'every sinew of the body' – if the exercises involve all muscles, they must be very rigorous, as it is hard to reach every muscle. • they make you extraordinarily strong: 'fell oxen ... with a single blow' – an ox is a huge, strong creature that is not easy to kill, so having the strength to defeat an ox with bare hands shows how strong the exercises make you. • they make you contort your body: 'not dignified' – exercises that work the whole body and are not dignified must lead to contortions of the body. • they look ridiculous: 'markedly humorous' – the sudden body contortions that the exercises involve are obviously so extreme that they look ridiculous; seeing someone strain with their body tied in knots can be funny, as it is unexpected. • they would make someone who is very depressed smile: 'only reason why King Henry… never smiled again' – to say that someone who lost their son would smile just watching the exercises suggests they are almost a comedy routine that would cheer everyone up. (Although all quotes are exaggerated descriptions, the basic message is true.)

LEVEL 1

Question	Type and structure	Answer possibilities
1(a) When are you allowed to run or jump in London?	**Recall** 2 marks – 1 mark per point made: one must be to do with jump, one with run	run: • after an omnibus • after a hat jump: • to avoid a taxi-cab • because you've stepped on a banana skin
1(b) When are you not?	**Recall** 2 marks – 1 mark per point made	• run to develop your lungs • jump because it's good for the liver
2(a) Three humorous quotations	**Technique (split)** **Evidence (3 marks)** 1 mark per appropriate quotation	• 'It rallies round and points the finger of scorn' • 'two cabman (one intoxicated)' • 'four waiters from the Hotel Mathis; six waiters from the Hotel Previtali' • 'They all laughed even the cat' • 'expel by means of physical fatigue a small devil of discontent' • 'The only reason why King Henry of England, whose son sank with the White Ship, never smiled again, was because Lieutenant Larsen had not then invented his admirable Exercises.'
2(b) Explain your choices	**Explanation (3 marks)** 1 mark per brief explanation	(In same order as the quotations above.) • the metaphor of London pointing out and making fun of someone who exercises, like children might, is funny as it is an overreaction to a harmless action. • the information in the brackets is unnecessary, but it adds humour as it suggests that Ashe doing his exercises is the kind of thing a drunkard would enjoy watching. • that both hotel staff watch is already humorous, as they stop all work to watch one man exercise. That the exact number of each type of employee is mentioned and set against each other, as though the hotels are rivals to watch Ashe, adds to the comic effect, as it is exaggerated. • the cat would not really be laughing, and the suggestion it does is exaggerated and sounds ridiculous, leading to humour. It also reminds of cartoon cats laughing, which adds to the humour. • the alliteration used in this phrase is humorous, as it makes the problem sound less than it is; by making the phrase sound slightly ridiculous (through short and fast alliteration), the author adds humour. • saying that watching someone go through a fitness regime would make someone who had lost their son laugh is so enormous an exaggeration that it is comic. The quotation also makes us realise how ridiculous the exercises must look.

Question	Type and structure	Answer possibilities
3 How does Ashe make people accept his fitness regime?	**Recall** 4 marks – 1 mark per point made	• through patience • through perseverance • by not letting himself be put off by the laughter • by staying calm • by continuing to do his exercises regularly for a month, by which time only children watch • by keeping on doing the exercises for three months, when they are accepted
4 What kind of a person is Ashe?	**Thought** 6 marks – 3 PEELs Per PEEL, 1 mark for point and evidence, 1 mark for brief explanation	• confident: 'whirled his Indian clubs' – although Londoners make fun of people doing exercise, he goes out onto the street to keep fit, showing he is confident enough to face people laughing at him. • determined: 'a month later' – although people laughed at him for exercising, he does not give up and keeps exercising until the neighbours accept him. • smartly dressed and well-off: 'sweater, flannel trousers' – although shorts would not have been wide-spread for exercise in those days, he sounds smartly dressed, as flannel trousers are finer material, suggesting he takes care of his appearance and is quite well-off. • believes that exercise can help: 'wished to expel by means of physical fatigue a small devil of discontent' – he is troubled in his mind and exercises to calm himself, which shows he believes fitness is the answer to most problems. • focused: 'measured and solemn fashion' – he breathes out slowly and seriously before starting his exercises, which shows that he is focused, getting into 'exercise mode' where nothing will disturb him.
5 What do you learn about Larsen Exercises?	**Recall** 5 marks – 1 mark per point made Can also be treated as **Thought** 5 marks – 2–3 PEELs	• they are the best exercise there is ('last word in exercises') • they work out the whole body ('bring into play every sinew of the body') • they increase your health ('promote a brisk circulation') • they make you strong ('fell oxen … with a single blow') • they make you look ridiculous ('they are not dignified') • they are so unusual, that you will make people laugh when you do them ('markedly humorous') (For suggestions on how to answer the question as a thought question, see level 2 on page 19.)

A Joust

LEVEL 2

Question	Type and Structure	Answer Possibilities
1 Describe the 'sweeping stroke'	**Recall** 2 marks – 1 mark per point made Must be own words	• instead of the lance pointing straight ahead you hold it so it is pointing across to the left, like a bar • that way you will definitely sweep your opponent off his horse
2 Describe the phases of the joust	**Recall** 4 points – 1 mark per point made	• they charge the first time, aiming for each other's heads • they both miss spectacularly • they rearrange themselves • they charge again, going for the sweeping stroke • both are unseated
3(a) How does the author bring the battle to life?	**Technique** 6 marks – 3 PEELs Per PEEL, 1 mark for point and evidence, 1 mark for explanation	• onomatopoeia: 'hurtle' – the dull 'ur' sound suggests something heavy moving and the trip of the tongue over the 'tle' suggests speed that almost overreaches itself, giving an idea of a looming collision. • metaphor: 'toned down into slow motion' – the charge has the same power and action as a fast charge, but seems slowed down, making it seem more inexorable as there would be time to act, but there isn't. • describing detail 'ponderous horses lumbered' – the weight of the horses and riders is emphasised here (ponderous, lumbered) and you have the feeling the horses can hardly walk, making the battle seem almost ridiculous. • onomatopoeia: 'clank, rumble, thump-thump' – the author is describing the sounds of the charge: the clank of the metal armour moving, the rumble of the earth as the horses hit it and the thump-thump of the hooves on the ground; the last three sounds are all dull, suggesting a slow roll of thunder as the two heavy horses move towards each other. • metaphor: 'blood–curdling beat of iron hoofs' – the coming together of the knights is so frightening in its power the blood almost stops flowing in apprehension. • onomatopoeia: 'thundered' – the dull heavy sound of both knights is like thunder rolling, the dark 'un' sound suggests the boom and the double 'd' sound at the end the reverberations of the thunder. • simile: 'like a motor omnibus in collision with a smithy' – an omnibus is huge and slow and made of metal, rather like the knights on horseback and a smithy is a small shed filled with iron objects, meaning the collision between the two would sound very metallic, but also be hefty.

Question	Type and Structure	Answer Possibilities
3(b) How do the Wart's comments add tension?	**Technique** 4 marks – 2 PEELs Per PEEL, 1 mark for point and evidence, 1 mark for explanation	• Comments are like a sports commentator, helping us to see the action and giving us an emotional depth to the happenings. • 'They're off!' – the excitement of the beginning of the joust is mirrored in the short phrase and the exclamation mark. • 'Now!' – this marks the moment when the horses clash, giving the reader a feeling of being present at the moment the knights come together. • 'Is it safe to look?' – fact that Wart had his eyes shut shows what a frightening spectacle the two knights charging is and brings this across for the reader. • 'I hope they don't hurt themselves' – for all the comical description and slow motion this comment reinforces that jousting is dangerous and the knights could kill each other.
4 Examples of humour	**Technique** 4 marks – 2 PEELs Per PEEL, 1 mark for point and evidence, 1 mark for explanation	• 'toned down into slow motion' – contrast between conventional representations of jousts as fast-paced, dashing battles and a slowed down version of the same with enormous weight-carrying horses is comical, as it deflates expectation. • 'splendid animals had shambled into an earth-shaking imitation of a trot' – alliteration adds to comic effect of horses not even being able to trot; contrast between splendid and shambled heightens humour and earth-shaking helps to give scene a feeling of weight contrary to the fleet attack we would expect. • 'flapping their elbows and legs in unison' – sounds like the knights are trying to take off as they desperately try to gain speed; the image of stately knights flapping ridiculously like chickens is funny, as unexpected. • 'drove his spear deep into the beech tree' – the ridiculous end to the lethal charge is funny. It is undignified and not in keeping with the high ideas of a joust that the lance ends in a tree. • 'omnibus' – comparing a knight in armour to an omnibus is unusual; as a large and lumbering hulk of metal it once again deflates the idea that knights were the sleek racing cars of their days; an omnibus is also a common mode of transport, while a knight should be refined.
5 Does the description of a joust differ from your expectations?	**Response** 5 marks – according to quality of response 1–2: simple response that shows little reference to the text and little thought 3–4: good, solid response with some reference to the text and some coherent points, with examples 5: sophisticated piece using elements from the text and points backed up with examples throughout	Answers will vary. Reference should be made to possibly unexpected elements, like weight of horse and rider, type of horse, speed of encounter, sweeping stroke. Reality of this could be questioned (is it humorous exaggeration?)

English for Common Entrance Answer Book

LEVEL 1

Question	Type and Structure	Answer Possibilities
1 What is the 'sweeping stroke'?	**Recall** 2 marks – 1 mark per point made	• instead of the lance pointing straight ahead you hold it at right angles toward the left, like a bar • that way you will definitely sweep your opponent off his horse
2 Describe the four phases of the battle	**Recall** 4 marks – 1 mark per point made	• they charge the first time, aiming for each other's heads • they both miss spectacularly • they charge again, going for the sweeping stroke • both are unseated
3(a) Note down one example each of a simile and onomatopoeia	**Technique (split)** **Evidence** 2 marks – 1 mark per appropriate quotation	Simile: • 'like a motor omnibus in collision with a smithy' Onomatopoeia: • thumping • clank, rumble, thump-thump • thundered • blundering • clang!
3(b) Explain the effect of each in detail	**Explanation** 4 marks – 2 marks per explanation; simple explanation will get 1 mark	(In the same order as the quotations above.) Simile: • an omnibus is huge and slow and made of metal, rather like the knights on horseback and a smithy is a small shed filled with iron objects, meaning the collision between the two would sound very metallic, but also be hefty. Onomatopoeia: • the hard, sudden 'p' sound suggests a hit and the dull 'um' shows it to be a more muffled sound, like hitting a body with a blunt object; here the knights are hitting their heels against the horses' sides, producing a sound like a thump. • the author is describing the sounds of the charge: the clank of the metal armour moving, the rumble of the earth as the horses hit it and the thump-thump of the hooves on the ground; the last three sounds are all dull, suggesting a slow roll of thunder as the two heavy horses move towards each other. • the dull heavy sound of both knights is like thunder rolling, the dark 'un' sound suggests the boom and the double 'd' sound at the end the reverberations of the thunder. • the 'bl' at the beginning suggests heaviness or even confusion as the horses charge. The dark 'un' sound mirrors the sound of their hooves on the ground, as do the repeated 'd' sounds at the end. So while the charge is noisy, there is some confusion about it. • this is a simple sound effect that mirrors the slightly bright hit of wood to metal as the lances hit the armour. It is a hard, sharp sudden sound that is quite hollow, mirroring the men in their armour being hit.

Question	Type and Structure	Answer Possibilities
4(a) Three examples of humour	**Technique (split)** **Evidence** 3 marks – 1 mark per appropriate quotation	• 'toned down into slow motion' • 'majestically, the ponderous horses lumbered into a walk' • 'splendid animals had shambled into an earth-shaking imitation of a trot' • 'flapping their elbows and legs in unison' • 'drove his spear deep into the beech tree' • 'omnibus'
4(b) Explain the humour briefly	**Explanation** 3 marks – 1 mark per brief explanation	(In the same order as the quotations above.) • the contrast between our imagination of jousts as fast-paced, dashing battles and a slowed down version of the same with enormous weight-carrying horses is comical. • majestically suggests gracefully, but to lumber is to walk slowly and heavily, building a humorous contrast. • the alliteration adds to comic effect of the horses not even being able to trot; something splendid should be able to do more than shamble; that it can't is funny. • this sounds like the knights are trying to take off as they try to speed up; the image of stately knights flapping ridiculously like chickens is unexpected. • the ridiculous end to the charge is funny. Instead of spearing his opponent, Grummore spears a tree, which is slapstick comedy. • 'omnibus' – comparing a knight in armour to an omnibus takes down the idea that knights were the sleek racing cars of their days.
5 Does the description of a joust differ from your expectations?	**Response** 4 marks – according to quality of response 1: simple response that shows little reference to the text and little thought 2–3: good, solid response with some reference to the text and some coherent, individual points, with some examples 4: engaging piece using elements from the text and personal points backed up with examples	Answers will vary. Reference should be made to possibly unexpected elements, like weight of horse and rider, type of horse, speed of encounter, sweeping stroke. Reality of this could be questioned (is it humorous exaggeration?)

The Power of Words

LEVEL 2

Question	Type and structure	Answer possibilities
1 How does Mrs Finucane make money? Own words	**Recall** 3 marks – 1 mark per point made Must be own words	• gives people tickets to buy clothes (meaning she pays for the clothes) • receives a discount but charges full price for the clothes • also charges interest for the money lent
2 How does Frank make the letters threatening	**Technique** 6 marks – 3 PEELs Per PEEL, 1 mark for point and evidence, 1 mark for explanation	• using complicated words: 'litigious' – Frank is writing to poor and simple people; by using complicated words he barely knows he is trying to sound more important and therefore threatening. • using threats: 'I may be forced to resort to legal action' – by outlining the consequences of not heeding the letter, it appears better to do as the letter says. • appeal to higher authorities: 'barrister above in Dublin' – by pretending to have a lawyer in the capital city, Frank is making Mrs Finucane sound more powerful and able to do more damage than she is or can. • giving concrete examples: 'There's your son, Michael' – this suggests she knows the addressee in detail, suggesting she is either watching them or knows their financial situation, too. • emotional appeal: 'far from friends and family' – by outlining the consequences of not paying in emotional terms, the letter gains power; people would not want to be away from the people they love most; the alliteration serves to emphasise this. • hyperbole: 'languish in the dungeons' – the word dungeons suggests subterranean caverns with no light, manacles and chains and little to no fresh food. While jail would not have been comfortable in those days, calling them dungeons is clearly an exaggeration.

Question	Type and structure	Answer possibilities
3 In what way does the extract show words have power	**Thought** 4 marks – 2 PEELs Per PEEL, 1 mark for point and evidence, 1 mark for explanation	• long words frighten: 'inasmuch, that's a holy terror of a word' – short words are usually simple like most people would use; using longer words that are rarer make people scared because their length makes them more difficult to avoid. • the sound of words can frighten: 'succumbed' – although used incorrectly here, the sound of the word, usually used in connection with illness and death, gives the letter a negative tone that reaches beyond the meaning of the words. • unknown words can frighten: 'a holy terror of a word. What does it mean?' – words that are long and complicated sound threatening especially if their meaning is unclear. They suggest that the reader is not as intelligent as the writer, giving the writer power. • most people pay immediately: 'four of 'em paid' – of the six letters he writes four pay immediately. They obviously feel powerless faced with such difficult and long words. • the letters reduce Mrs O'Brien to tears: 'She came in tremblin' with tears in her eyes' – although she ignored the first letter, the second one with more long words than short, frightens her so much that she pays. This also shows that words have different degrees of power as the first letter did not work. • words are indelible: 'Put the fear of God in 'em' – spoken words would not be as effective, as they disappear once spoken. Written words are more powerful as they remain on the page and will not go away. They can be read and read again (especially when not readily understood), increasing their power.
4 Impressions of the author	**Thought** 6 marks – 3 PEELs Per PEEL, 1 mark for point and evidence, 1 mark for explanation	• thrifty: 'Why should I squander money on stamps' – although he has been given money for the stamps he decides to keep it and deliver the letters on foot instead, which is more onerous. For him money is more important, as he is saving up to go to America and he will use any opportunity to save money. • ashamed of his work for Mrs Finucane: 'praying no one will see me' – he knows that he is threatening poor people who have no money to spare – people like him – and he is not proud of what he is doing, so he hopes no one will see him. • determined: 'bring your own paper and envelopes' – although he is poor, he obviously gets his own paper and envelopes to be able to get the job, showing he is determined and will let nothing stop him. • proud of his abilities: 'I begin to throw in words I hardly understand myself' – he is pleased with what his letters can do and he embellishes them more and more, almost showing off the words he can think up. • mercenary: 'I'm desperate for that job' – although he knows what he is doing is not right, he still does it because he wants to earn enough money so he can go to America. This suggests he will do almost any job to gain money – even running through Limerick late at night to save stamp money.

Question	Type and structure	Answer possibilities
5 How does the author bring the passage to life	**Technique** 6 marks – 3 PEELs Per PEEL, 1 mark for point and evidence, 1 mark for explanation	• dialogue: 'Threaten 'em by' – reading the actual words the people say makes the story more direct. Here, the dialogue is in dialect, making it sound even more realistic. The lack of speech marks embeds the words directly in the story, making them more immediate. • short paragraphs: 'I run through the lanes of Limerick … will see me' – the action is simply described and moves swiftly on. The short paragraphs move the story along more quickly, like him running through the lanes. • powerful verbs: 'squander' – although he is only talking of buying six stamps, so obviously not a huge amount of money, he calls spending it wasting it, showing he cannot afford to lose even such a small amount of money. • quoting the letters verbatim: lines 17–23 and 35–37 – the detail of the exact words of the letters Frank writes helps us understand what he is talking about and helps us relive his pride as well as the addressees' terrors when faced with such letters. • repetition: 'sharper and sharper' – the repetition shows the progress of the letters. From week to week McCourt improves the letters and continues working on the words, which the repetition suggests. • alliteration: 'the lanes of Limerick shoving letters' – the repetition of the ' ' sound makes this more memorable and also suggests a loping or lilting gait as he runs through the streets.

LEVEL 1

Question	Type and structure	Answer possibilities
1 Why might people go to Mrs. Finucane for money?	**Recall** 4 marks – 1 mark per point made	• they need to buy something • they don't • Mrs Finucane will give them the money • they pay her back in small, afferdable installments
2(a) Quotations that are persuasive	**Technique (split)** **Evidence** 2 marks – 1 mark per appropriate quotation	• 'I may be forced to resort to legal action' • 'There's your son, Michael' • 'far from friends and family' • 'I myself have barely a crust to keep body and soul together' • 'languish in the dungeons'
2(b) Explain your choices in detail	**Explanation** 4 marks – 2 marks per explanation; simple explanation will get 1 mark	(In the same order as the quotations above.) • by outlining what will happen if she doesn't pay and threatening taking her to court it appears better to do as the letter says. • addressing the recipient directly and giving a concrete example suggests Mrs Finucane knows a lot about the family of the addressee and is watching them to make sure she gets her money. • by saying if she doesn't pay she will lose those she loves most, the letter is appealing to Mrs O'Brien's sense of family and her feelings for them and her friends. • pretending Mrs Finucane has no food because she has given all her money to other people who don't repay her and let her starve is an attempt to make Mrs O'Brien feel guilty about not paying the money back. • the word dungeons suggests underground caves with no light, where people are chained to the walls and starved. Jail would not have been like this, so the letter is trying to scare people into thinking what will happen is worse than it actually will be.
3 In what way are the given phrases powerful?	**Thought (simplified)** **Explanation** 5 marks – 1 mark per brief explanation	All words are long and complicated making the reader who does not understand them feel less intelligent and powerful than the writer. • inasmuch: this suggests that something bad is going to follow the word. • litigious anticipation: litigation has to do with courts, so this sounds like Mrs Finucane is looking forward to going to court, which means she knows she's right. • imminence of litigation: this sounds like going to courts is going to happen very soon, almost immediately, which would frighten the addressee. • epistle: this makes the letter sound more important, almost like a book of the Bible (the letters in the New Testament are usually called epistles). • in consultation with our barrister: barrister suggests that the matter is already in court and consultation suggests that something is happening in close contact and cooperation with the barrister.

English for Common Entrance Answer Book

Question	Type and structure	Answer possibilities
4 What kind of person is the author?	**Thought** 2 + 4 marks – 2 PEELs Per PEEL, 1 mark for point and evidence, 2 marks for explanation; simple explanation will get 1 mark	• thrifty: 'Why should I squander money on stamps' – although he has been given money for the stamps he decides to keep it and deliver the letters on foot instead, showing he will use any opportunity to save money. • ashamed of his work for Mrs Finucane: 'praying no one will see me' – he knows that he is threatening poor people who have no money with prison. He is not proud of what he is doing, so he hopes no one will see him. • proud of his abilities: 'I begin to throw in words I hardly understand myself' – he is pleased with what his letters can do and he uses more and more complicated words, almost showing off the words he can think up. • will do anything for money: 'I'm desperate for that job' – although he knows what he is doing is not right, he still does it because he wants to earn enough money so he can go to America. He also runs through Limerick at night to keep the stamp money.
5 How does the author make his difficult childhood clear	**Technique** 4 marks – 2 PEELs Per PEEL, 1 mark for point and evidence, 1 mark for simple explanation	• short sentences: 'I'm desperate for that job' – simple statement underlines how important job is for McCourt. The fact that he needs a job shows he is poor and he does not have much money. • powerful verbs: 'squander' – if he calls spending the money for stamps squandering, which means wasting, then he must be poor as this would not be that much money. • describing detail: 'When you're poor' – to be able to describe what it's like being poor, he must know something about it, suggesting he is poor. • alliteration: 'running through the lanes of Limerick' – the repetition of the 'l' sound is rolling, showing the speed of his running. That he has to run shows he is not well off as he has no other way of moving large distances about the town. • writing his thoughts: 'praying no-one will see me' - he doesn't want to be seen and blamed, as he is poor himself, but working against other poor people. He has to betray his own class to get on in the world.

Journey to Castle Dracula

LEVEL 2

Question	Type and structure	Answer possibilities
1(a) What mood is created in the first paragraph?	**Thought** 1 mark – 1 mark for appropriate point	• one of claustrophobia • being hemmed in • being closed in (tension alone is not sufficient as answer)
1(b) How does the author create the mood?	**Technique** 6 marks – 3 PEELs Per PEEL, 1 mark for point and evidence, 1 mark for explanation	• repetition: 'nearer and nearer' – if the wolves are approaching ever closer, this adds to a feeling of being closed in because the closer the wolves are, the less room you have to manoeuvre. • simile: 'as through a tunnel' – a tunnel is a long, dark tube which does not let you go right or left, only a narrow straight ahead, which adds to the feeling of being closed in as there is only one way to go, all others being blocked off. • metaphor: 'frowning rocks guarded' – if you are being guarded, your freedom to move and do what you want is reduced; that the rocks are frowning suggests they are not friendly guards, so will keep the narrator close. • metaphor: 'covered with a white blanket' – a blanket is a thick covering that lets nothing through; although a blanket can keep warm and protect, is can also smother and the emphasis here is on this. • choice of verb: 'hemmed in' – describing the actual situation makes it clear; hemming in is sewing cloth around tightly so it can't escape to fray; this suggests here that the trees are close and tight around the coach, adding to a sense of being closed in. • describing detail: 'I could not see anything through the darkness' – not being able to see what's around you cuts you off from the outside world and closes you in on yourself, heightening a sense of claustrophobia, of being surrounded by black, impenetrable walls.
2 What does the driver do when he spots a blue flame?	**Recall** 3 marks – 1 mark per point made	• stops horses/ carriage • goes quickly over to where the flame is • marks the spot with stones

Question	Type and structure	Answer possibilities
3 What makes you think the coachman is not normal?	**Thought** 6 marks – 3 PEELs Per PEEL, 1 mark for point and evidence, 1 mark for explanation	• he can obviously see in darkness: 'He kept turning his head to left and right, but I could not see anything through the darkness' – normally you only turn your head if there is something to see. Harker cannot see anything, suggesting it is pitch black. The fact that the driver obviously can see things in this darkness suggests he is not quite normal. • the driver abandons the coach at night when there are wolves around: 'disappeared into the darkness' – as a coach driver you are responsible for the safety of the passengers. Leaving the coach in the middle of the night in wolf territory is not what a normal driver would do. In addition he abandons it for a long time. • the driver does not talk: 'without a word' – it would be customary for the coachman to exchange at least a few words with his passenger, especially to calm him in a situation as that described. The driver does nothing of the kind, suggesting he is not ordinary. • He stops the journey to look at blue flames: 'he went rapidly to where the blue flame rose' – stopping the coach when wolves are surrounding it seems reckless already, but to stop just to look at a blue flame seems very strange and inexplicable and certainly not the actions of a normal man; a normal driver would not stop and certainly not for a blue flame. • he seems to be translucent: 'when he stood between me and the flame he did not obstruct it' – normally if you stand in front of a flame, the flame would be hidden; despite the driver being between Harker and the flame, Harker can still see the fire, which is unusual and suggests the driver may not be as solid as he appears. • seems to be able to walk among wolves: 'howling of the wolves drew closer' – they are surrounded by wolves and yet the driver stops the coach and disappears into the night, seemingly unaffected by the wolves in close proximity; a normal human being would avoid a pack of wolves if at all possible, but he doesn't, emphasising his strangeness.

Question	Type and structure	Answer possibilities
4 In what way do the wolves add to the tension?	**Thought** 6 marks – 3 PEELs Per PEEL, 1 mark for point and evidence, 1 mark for explanation	In all cases: wolves are predators that hunt in packs and will kill a human being. The climate being cold it can be assumed the wolves would be hungry and chase and kill the horses and/or Harker, if given a chance. This threat of imminent death heightens the tension in each case. • accompany the coach: 'baying of the wolves sounded nearer and nearer' – the fact that the wolves chase the coach suggests they have singled it out as potential prey, or at least want to check it out to see whether it might make an easy killing. • surround it as it drives: 'as though they were closing round on us from every side' or 'following in a moving circle' – predators hunting in packs classically single out their prey by surrounding it, so it can't escape, and then go in to attack and then kill it. That the coach is surrounded suggests the wolves will, at some point, attack the horses. • draw closer as coach stops: 'the howling of the wolves drew closer' – the coach stopping might signal to wolves that their prey is exhausted, so they move in for the attack and kill. • they guard the coach in menacing silence: 'I saw around us a ring of wolves' – the silence of the circling wolves suggests they are full of grim purpose. They have made up their minds and are now going to jump at the horses.
5 Effectiveness of having a first person narrator	**Response** 3 marks – according to quality of response 1: simple response that shows little thought 2: good, solid response with some reference to the text 3: engaging piece using elements from the text and points backed up with examples	Answers will vary. Reference should be made to immediacy of first person narrative, heightened credibility of first person, limited knowledge of Harker's pov, that reader can only see and experience what Harker does.

English for Common Entrance Answer Book

LEVEL 1

Question	Type and structure	Answer possibilities
1 What does the driver do when he sees a blue flame?	**Recall** 3 marks – 1 mark per point made	• stops horses/carriage • goes quickly over to where the flame is • marks the spot with stones
2(a) Three quotations that create a claustrophobic mood	**Technique (split)** **Evidence** 3 marks – 1 mark per appropriate quotation	• 'nearer and nearer' • 'as through a tunnel' • 'frowning rocks guarded' • 'covered with a white blanket' • 'hemmed in' • 'I could not see anything through the darkness'
2(b) Explain the effect of two of these quotations	**Explanation** 4 marks – 2 marks per explanation; simple explanation will get 1 mark	(In the same order as the quotations above.) • the repetition tells us the wolves are approaching ever closer, which adds to a feeling of being closed in because the closer the wolves are, the less room you have to manoeuvre. • a tunnel is a long, dark tube which does not let you go right or left, only straight ahead. The simile therefore adds to the feeling of being closed in as there is only one way to go. • if you are being guarded by unfriendly guards (the rocks are frowning), your freedom to move and do what you want is reduced; the metaphor therefore suggests limited space to move. • a blanket is a thick covering that lets nothing through; when covered like that you cannot move easily so this metaphor suggests a feeling of being closed in. • describing the actual situation makes it clear; when you are hemmed in you can't move so the trees here are close and tight around the coach. • not being able to see what's around you cuts you off from the outside world, making you think you are surrounded by walls of black night.
3(a) Clues that suggest the driver is not normal	**Thought (split)** **Evidence** 2 marks – 1 mark per appropriate quotation	• 'He kept turning his head to left and right, but I could not see anything through the darkness' • 'disappeared into the darkness' • 'he went rapidly to where the blue flame rose' • 'when he stood between me and the flame he did not obstruct it'

Question	Type and structure	Answer possibilities
3(b) Explain your choices in detail	**Explanation** 4 marks – 2 marks per explanation; simple explanation will get 1 mark	(In the same order as the quotations above.) • he can obviously see in darkness as you only turn your head if there is something to see. It is pitch black, but the driver can still see, making him not quite normal. • the driver abandons the coach at night when there are wolves around, which is not normal because as a coach driver you are responsible for the safety of the passengers. In addition he abandons it for a long time. • he stops the journey to look at blue flames when wolves are surrounding it. Merely stopping with wolves around is dangerous, but to stop just to look at a blue flame seems very strange. • normally if you stand in front of a flame, the flame would be hidden; although the driver is between Harker and the flame, Harker can still see the fire, which is unusual and suggests the driver is somehow see-through.
4(a) Three ways in which the wolves scare the narrator	**Thought (split)** **Evidence** 3 marks – 1 mark per appropriate quotation	• 'baying of the wolves sounded nearer and nearer, as though they were closing round on us from every side' • 'following in a moving circle' • 'the howling of the wolves drew closer' • 'I saw around us a ring of wolves'
4(b) Explain in what way each incident creates tension	**Explanation** 3 marks – 1 mark per brief explanation	In all cases: wolves are predators that hunt in packs and can kill a human being or the horses, so the fact that they are close leads to an atmosphere of danger. • they accompany the coach which suggests they have singled it out as potential prey. • they surround the carriage as it drives, so it can't escape. • as soon as the coach stops they draw closer meaning they are moving in for the attack and kill. • the silence of the wolves standing around the coach suggests they are full of grim purpose. They have made up their minds and are now going to jump at the horses.
5 Is the story more effective with a first person narrator?	**Response** 3 marks – according to quality of response 1: simple response that shows little thought 2: good, solid response with some reference to the text and some individual points 3: engaging piece using elements from the text and personal points	Answers will vary. Reference could be made to immediacy of first person narrative, heightened credibility of first person, limited knowledge of Harker's pov, that reader can only see and experience what Harker does.

'Stealing'

LEVEL 2

Question	Type and structure	Answer possibilities
1 Effect of the poem starting and ending with a question	**Technique** 3 marks – 1 mark per point made	• interaction with audience • challenges reader • gains interest • last question tries to excuse his behaviour, that no one can relate to him, tries to turn him into victim
2 Why has the poet included 'Aah'?	**Thought** 2 marks – either two points or one more detailed explanation	• onomatopoeia makes the scene vivid (actually using sound the narrator makes) • shows how self-centred he is (mirror makes him go Aah): he is obviously pleased with himself • exhalation gives a sense of relief/freedom/worth from actions
3 What kind of language does the poet use?	**Technique** 4 marks – 2 PEELs Per PEEL, 1 mark for point and evidence, 1 mark for explanation	• onomatopoeia: 'slice of ice' – the sharp and hard 's' sound sounds like sharp draw of breath when something is cold, so it recreates the coldness of his mind and the snow. • colloquial turns of phrase: 'mate', 'daft' or 'pinch' suggest someone talking directly and shows his social background: he cannot be bothered to use standard English and may not be able to speak it. • random topics: snowman, stealing, breaking in suggest stream of consciousness, we are party to narrator's thoughts; thoughts classically don't move logically, but in jumps, as they do here. • one word bursts emphasise the factors involved in his life and also suggest stream of consciousness.
4 Relevance of the guitar and Shakespeare bust	**Thought** 4 marks – 2 PEELs Per PEEL, 1 mark for point and evidence, 1 mark for explanation	• 'thought I might/ earn to play' – guitar shows how he doesn't finish anything. Not committed enough to actually sit down and learn. Wants to escape boredom but does not have the self-discipline. • 'nicked a bust of Shakespeare' – correlates in part to the three parts of the snowman. Represents intellectual challenge that narrator is not prepared to engage with – he just thinks of money. Shakespeare stands for hard way of slow learning: narrator only interested in easy cash. A creative social genius is contrasted with anti-social destructive character of the narrator.

Question	Type and structure	Answer possibilities
5 Why did the narrator steal the snowman and why is he telling the story?	**Thought** 6 marks – 3 PEELs Per PEEL, 1 mark for point and evidence, 1 mark for explanation	• narrator can identify with snowman: 'mute' – the snowman cannot talk and the narrator feels he has no voice, either. Like the snowman he is only physically there, not integrated into society. • shows futility of narrator's life: 'alone amongst lumps of snow' – stealing something that's difficult to steal and absolutely worthless shows that narrator doesn't even have a purpose to his criminal activity, but anything seems better than boredom. • shows sheer spite of narrator: 'Part of the thrill was knowing/that children would cry' – the narrator's purpose in stealing the snowman is not to own something, but to hurt others through his theft. • adrenalin rush: 'fierce chill' – stealing things gives the narrator a kick and he needs to do these things to get the rush that he is hooked on. • wanted the snowman, but failed: 'Reassembled in the yard,/he didn't look the same' – thief cannot make snowman look the same as children, so destroys it. Shows he prefers to destroy when things don't work out like he wants, than build anything of his own.
6 How can you tell that the narrator does not share the values of society?	**Thought** 6 marks – 3 PEELs Per PEEL, 1 mark for point and evidence, 1 mark for explanation	• defines living differently: 'better off dead' – identifies own moral structure, that taking what you want to take is acceptable. Anything is allowed to feel alive and to beat boredom. • enjoys hurting others: 'part of the thrill' – narrator steals with the full knowledge that his actions will upset the victims. Identifies the cruelty and selfishness of his actions. • does not want to come into physical contact: 'gloved hand' – image of barrier between thief and society; he does not want to get his hands dirty on society or be infected by it – although he is the dangerous element. • doesn't really exist: 'ghost' – he does not feel a full member of society and tries not to leave traces. He is happier unnoticed. • isolated: 'alone' – due to what he does he is alone as his actions are not social. Friends would not support that kind of action. • feels left out: 'sick of the world' – this shows he does not know what to do in the social world, it makes him sick, he has no place in it.

LEVEL 1

Question	Type and structure	Answer possibilities
1(a) Why does the poem start with a question?	**Thought** 2 marks – reward any suggestion with up to 2 marks depending on detail	• engages the reader • makes the reader think someone is talking to him • makes it seem like the reader is listening in on a conversation • makes it sound informal • shows the narrator is thinking about the answer
1(b) Why does the poem end with a question?	**Thought** 2 marks – reward any suggestion with up to 2 marks depending on detail	• it's a bit of a joke: we don't understand the poem and the narrator says we don't understand it. • shows that the narrator is not really interested in the reader's reaction. • shows how different the narrator's world is to ours. • makes the reader question everything that's been said.
2 Why does the poet use short phrases?	**Thought (simplified)** 4 marks – mark any one suggestion with up to 2 marks, depending on detail	• shows that the narrator does not think a lot about his answers • shows narrator's impulsiveness: his life is a burst of activity and emotions • he doesn't have a lot of time to talk • he finds talking boring • he does not have a very good education, so can't express himself well
3 Name four things the narrator has stolen	**Recall** 4 marks – 1 mark per object mentioned	• snowman • camera • guitar • bust of Shakespeare
4 What makes the stealing of the snowman unusual?	**Thought** 2 + 4 marks – 2 PEELs Per PEEL, 1 mark for point and evidence, 2 marks for explanation; simple explanation will get 1 mark	• 'a mate': sees the snowman as a friend rather than an object – strange as you can't steal a friend and an object can't really be a friend. • 'looked magnificent': snowman is almost like a work of art, a great cultural achievement – while it's not unusual to want to steal art, the snowman isn't art; his magnificence depends on him being alone in the night, which is not something you can steal. • 'knowing that children would cry': he does not steal so much for his own gain as to hurt others – unusual as theft is usually the desire to possess, not the desire to take away or hurt. • 'booted him': destroys the snowman after having stolen him – usually a thief takes care of his stolen goods, but here he destroys it, making the theft pointless.
5 Quotes that show the narrator does not share the society's values	**Recall** 3 marks – 1 mark per relevant quote	• 'The most unusual thing I ever stole?' • 'Better off dead than ... not taking/what you want' • 'Part of the thrill was knowing/that children would cry in the morning' • 'I steal things I don't need' • 'I joy-ride cars' • 'break into houses' • 'pinch a camera' • 'nicked a bust of Shakespeare once'

Question	Type and structure	Answer possibilities
6 How does the author make us believe this is a thief talking?	**Technique** 4 marks – 2 PEELs Per PEEL, 1 mark for point and evidence, 1 mark for simple explanation	• use of colloquial language: 'nicked', 'flogged', 'daft' – more relaxed way of speaking and use of slang shows that the speaker is probably not educated; a common thief would not speak polished English. • jumping from topic to topic: 'One time, I stole a guitar' – when people speak they often jump from topic to topic; here the thief is reminiscing, so subject matter shifts. • adding detail to descriptions: 'Mirrors' – he is remembering his thefts. Short addition of detail suggests he goes through the scenes in his head. • use of hyperbole: 'I could eat myself' – such simple exaggerations are frequent with people who struggle to express themselves eloquently.

English for Common Entrance Answer Book

'The Thought-Fox'

LEVEL 2

Question	Type and structure	Answer possibilities
1 How does the poet make the night sound dreary?	**Technique** 6 marks – 3 PEELs Per PEEL, 1 mark for point and evidence, 1 mark for explanation	• metaphor: 'the clock's loneliness' – if even the inanimate can feel abandoned and left all alone, it is obviously a sad and gloomy night. • close description: 'blank page' – blank can also mean uneventful, suggesting the page is dull and uninspiring, which is another meaning of dreary. • close description/negatives: 'no star' – stars make the night beautiful and comforting, their lack (and the emphasis of no) suggests a dull night of no hope or softer emotions. • repetition: 'loneliness' (lines 3 and 8) – emphasising how stark and bare the night is suggests it is gloomy. • alliteration: 'deeper within darkness' – repetition of dull 'd' sound underlines the covering blackness of the night in which there is nothing.
2 Explain line 12	**Thought** 4 marks – 2 PEELs Per PEEL, 1 mark for point and evidence, 1 mark for explanation	• the repeated 'now' suggest something that is happening in the present, the same thing over and over – as this relates to the fox coming it is setting down of the footprints by the fox. • the repeated 'and' suggest a pause, or hesitance between the footfalls of the 'now' – the fox is moving warily, selecting carefully where it puts its paws. • 'again' emphasises the repetition that runs through this line – the fox is moving slowly, but smoothly, in a regular manner.
3 How can you tell that at the end of the poem something has changed in the night?	**Recall** 3 marks – 1 mark per point made	• although nothing seems to have changed from the beginning: the window is still 'starless' and the 'clock ticks', the other thing mentioned in the room, the paper, that was 'blank' in stanza one is now 'printed', so the change is that the paper now has words on it, something has been written.

Question	Type and structure	Answer possibilities
4 How does the poet make the fox come to life?	**Technique** 6 marks – 3 PEELs Per PEEL, 1 mark for point and evidence, 1 mark for explanation	• Alliteration: 'touches twig' or 'delicately ... dark' – the short, sharp 't' or 'd' sound imitates the careful touch of nose to objects, the d being slightly duller and softer than the t. • sibilance: 'sets neat prints into the snow' – soft hissing sound mirrors the treading in of fresh snow, that does not crunch, but crumbles with a gentle swish. • powerful adverbs: 'warily' – the word helps emphasise the caution with which the fox is proceeding and supports the other techniques. • alliteration: 'a lame/Shadow lags' – the rolling 'l' sound suggests a nonchalant, uneven gait, that moves hunched and in waves, like the shape of the tongue as it makes the 'l'. • metaphor: 'a widening deepening greenness' – this image of the eye coming closer suggests that somehow the forest (greenness) is captured in the fox's eye; it also suggests the gaze is mesmerising as it takes up the whole field of vision of the narrator. • use of the senses: 'hot stink of fox' – the smell of fox is very sharp and distinctive; using the adjective 'hot' suggests an attack on the nose that the scent of fox launches.
5 Is the poet writing about a real or an imaginary encounter?	**Thought** 6 marks – 3 PEELs Per PEEL, 1 mark for point and evidence, 1 mark for explanation Pupils can argue a mix, e.g. that there is a real fox, but that the poet enhances it through his imagination	Real: • 'coming about its own business' – the fox is independent and follows only its own business, suggesting it is real and not just imaginary. • 'something more near ... is entering the loneliness' – there has to be another being to enter the loneliness and break it, meaning the fox is real. • 'through the window I see' – it is very possible that the poet would be able to see a fox out of his window. Imaginary: • 'it enters the dark hole of the head' – the fox can't actually enter the poet's mind, but the fact that it does suggests it is imaginary. • 'window is starless still' – the still suggests that the view out of the window has not changed at all; this would mean there has been no fox (otherwise the poet would use 'again'). • 'hot stink', 'widening, deepening greenness' – the description is too detailed: the poet would not be able to get that close to a real fox, suggesting he is imagining it.

LEVEL 1

Question	Type and structure	Answer possibilities
1 Two quotations from lines 1–8 that show the night is dreary and explain the effect of end quotation	**Technique** 2 + 4 marks – 2 PEELs Per PEEL, 1 mark for point and evidence, 2 marks for explanation; simple explanation will get 1 mark	• 'the clock's loneliness' – if even a thing like a clock can feel left all alone, it is obviously a sad and gloomy night (metaphor). • 'blank page' – blank can also mean uneventful, suggesting the page is dull like the night (describing detail). • 'no star' – stars make the night beautiful and comforting; their lack makes the night dark and gloomy (negative/detailed description). • 'loneliness' (lines 3 and 8) – emphasising how all alone the narrator is suggests it is gloomy (repetition). • 'deeper within darkness' – repetition of dull 'd' sound underlines the dreariness of the night (alliteration).
2 How are the movements of the fox vivid in lines 11–14?	**Technique** 6 marks – 3 PEELs Per PEEL, 1 mark for point and evidence, 1 mark for explanation (need not be very detailed)	• repetition: 'and now' – suggests that the fox is putting its paws down slowly and carefully, as each separate 'and now' is a small movement. • describing detail: 'two eyes serve a movement' – suggests the eyes lead the fox as it moves and that the eyes move as the fox moves. • sibilance: 'sets neat prints into the snow' – sound is soft like the paws breaking through fresh snow. • describing detail: 'neat' – the fox is putting its feet down very carefully, not smudging its tracks. • adverb: 'warily' – underlines how cautiously the fox is moving, as though it knows it is being watched.
3 What has happened to the page at the end of the poem?	**Recall** 2 marks – one mark per point made	• at the beginning the page was 'blank' • at the end it is 'printed' meaning it has been written on (or typed upon)
4(a) Three quotations that describe the fox	**Thought (split)** **Evidence** 3 marks – 1 mark per appropriate quotation	• 'delicately ... /A fox's nose touches twig' • 'a lame/Shadow lags by stump' • 'a body that is bold' • 'an eye,/A widening deepening greenness' • 'sharp hot stink of fox'
4(b) What do the quotations tell you about the fox?	**Explanation** 3 marks – 1 mark per explanation	(In same order as the quotations above.) • it smells its surroundings carefully, orientating itself by scent. • it moves slowly, almost like a ghost, often stopping behind cover. • it is coloured very distinctly and can be surprisingly daring, coming out into the open. • its eyes are a bright green that reflects its woodland home. • it has a very strong, penetrating smell that is hurtful to the nose.
5 Explain line 22	**Thought** 5 marks – 1–2 marks per point made, depending on detail	• the fox the narrator has seen now takes hold of his imagination as it 'enters his head'. • the fox has found its den or a resting place in the head of the narrator/poet, suggesting it is not real. • the fox likes the dark and is seeking a dark hiding place. • there has never been a fox: the narrator has made it up out of the darkness of the night and it is now coming into the darkness of the narrator's head, meaning he is imagining it in detail.

From 'War Music'

LEVEL 2

Question	Type and structure	Answer possibilities
1 Who is the narrator addressing?	**Thought** 1 mark	Patroclus
2 Why did the poet choose the layout of 'Apollo!'?	**Thought** 4 marks – 2 PEELs Per PEEL, 1 mark for point and evidence, 1 mark for explanation	• highlights importance of Apollo: it's the only word on the page – Apollo is a god and therefore so important he fills a whole double page. • Apollo blots out all else: nothing else will fit next to the word – when the god appears before Patroclus he fills the entire field of vision of the hero, making him oblivious to all else, much like the reader's vision is filled with the one word. • Apollo is powerful: bold, large writing – the god is so superior to the human that his writing needs to be larger and fatter to emphasise this. • his appearance is surprising: a reader would not expect just one word splashed across a double page – Apollo appears unexpectedly, as evidenced by the exclamation mark, and the surprise of the reader at finding only one word on the page mirrors Patroclus's surprise at being confronted by the god.
3 How does the author make the wounding of Patroclus vivid?	**Technique** 8 marks – 4 PEELs Per PEEL, 1 mark for point and evidence, 1 mark for explanation	• powerful verb: 'eyes lurched out' – lurch suggests a sudden jolt and jumping out, meaning the blow to the helmet must have been forceful, nearly knocking Patroclus's eyes out. • tricolon: 'footless … staggering … amazed …' – the sudden strike of the god leaves Patroclus reeling, which is expressed in the tricolon, with the loss of balance slowly becoming a loss of thought – wonder and surprise. • ellipsis: 'footless … staggering … amazed …' – the pauses show how time seems to slow down as Patroclus realises he is wounded and the blow affects him. • paragraphing: 'Struck.' – the singling out of the one word makes it clear that this is a unique blow that is powerful. • onomatopoeia: 'rang' – the rolling 'r' at the beginning and the open 'ang' suggest a clatter and reverberation as the hit strikes home and makes the helmet resonate. Usually bells ring when struck forcibly and that a helmet does so here, suggests it was a mighty blow. • describing detail: 'vomit on your chest' – the blow was so strong that it made Patroclus involuntarily vomit, a very strong reaction that shows he is nauseous and dizzy from the blow.

Question	Type and structure	Answer possibilities
4 Explain the Trojans' reactions to Patroclus's wounding	**Thought** 6 marks – 3 PEELs Per PEEL, 1 mark for point and evidence, 1 mark for explanation	• they are amazed: 'lay and stared at you' – although many Trojans are dying, they muster enough strength to watch Patroclus die; 'stare' suggests surprise that this Greek hero would be felled so easily – or they are surprised at the appearance of Apollo. • can't believe what they are seeing: 'stared at you' – repetition of the staring suggests the Trojans find it hard to believe that the warrior who just cut a swathe through them is now felled himself. • they feel lucky: 'as blest as you felt cursed' – the sudden turn of events makes the Trojans feel that a god has heard their prayers and 'blest' them, coming to their aid. • they gather their courage: 'a hero boy called Thackta, cast' – encouraged by the fall of Patroclus, the Trojans rally and one of them, a boy to boot, throws his javelin at Patroclus; they feel that now Patroclus is wounded their situation is no longer hopeless.
5 Is the topic and style valid for poetry?	**Response** 6 marks – according to quality of response 1–2: simple response that shows little reference to the poem and little thought 3–4: good, solid response with some reference to the poem and some coherent points, with examples 5–6: sophisticated piece using elements from the poem and points backed up with examples throughout	Answers will vary. Reference should be made to the graphic imagery (e.g. 'dabbling … in the vomit') and whether this is something a poem should be dealing with. Pupils could also pick up on very straightforward style of description, as well as the fact that it is written in the 2nd person and how that makes the reader feel (does it make the violence more immediate and intimate, or more universal?). Pupils do not have to present both sides of the argument.

LEVEL 1

Question	Type and structure	Answer possibilities
1 Who is the poet talking to?	**Thought** 1 mark	Patroclus
2 Why has the single word Apollo been written across page?	**Thought** 4 marks – 1 mark per explanation or 2 marks for each more detailed explanation	• it shows how mighty Apollo is: the big, bold letters show that he is much stronger than all other people, who are in smaller print. • the big word surprises you: you don't expect just one word spread across the page – Apollo's appearance is surprising too. • there is no way to describe a god, but making his name stand out in big letters underlines it's a god, not a normal person who has come. • as the word takes up a whole line, so Apollo takes up the vision of Patroclus and the Trojans when he appears. • it makes the reader stop and stare like the fighters would at the appearance of a god. • it is almost like someone shouting: the appearance of the god is sudden and violent, like a shout; the exclamation mark at the end emphasises this.
3(a) Three effective quotes about the wounding of Patroclus	**Technique (split)** **Evidence** 3 marks – 1 mark per appropriate quotation	• 'Your eyes lurched out' • 'Achilles' bonnet rang' • 'footless… staggering'… amazed' • 'like weirs heard far away' • 'dabbling your astounded fingers/In the vomit on your chest'
3(b) Explain choice in detail	**Explanation** 6 marks – 2 marks per explanation; simple explanation will get 1 mark	(In the same order as the quotations above.) • lurch is jumping out at a sudden shock, so his eyes suddenly almost burst from his head as he is hit on the head (powerful verb). • bonnet means helmet and if it rings, it has obviously been hit hard and the metal still shakes from the shock (onomatopoeia). • Patroclus is moving almost in slow motion and is dazed after being hit so hard; he has been surprised and can't regain his balance due to the hit and amazement (tricolon or ellipsis). • his hearing has been affected and he hears things like waterfalls far away or as though he is underwater: his ears are buzzing softly, adding to his disorientation (simile). • he is unaware of his bodily reaction to the wounding as everything happened so fast: he is surprised to find he has vomited from the strength of the blow. Vomit shows extreme discomfort, underlining the strength of the blow (describing detail). • the javelin is long and thin and has pierced both legs, as though sewing them together; the simple description taken from a simple household task makes the violence seem even worse (metaphor).

Question	Type and structure	Answer possibilities
4(a) Three words that show the reaction of the Trojans	**Thought (split)** **Evidence** 3 marks – 1 mark per appropriate quotation	• 'lay and stared at you' • 'stared at you' • 'as blest as you felt cursed' • 'a hero boy called Thackta, cast'
4(b) What do they tell us about the Trojans	**Explanation** 3 marks – 1 mark per brief explanation	(In the same order as the quotations above.) • they are amazed • can't believe what they are seeing • they feel lucky • they gather their courage
5 Does such a description of a battle make a good poem?	**Response** 5 marks according to quality of response 1–2: simple response that shows little reference to the poem and little thought 3–4: good, solid response with some reference to the poem and some coherent, individual points, with some examples 5: engaging piece using elements from the poem and personal points backed up with examples	Answers will vary. Reference should be made to the graphic imagery (e.g. 'dabbling … in the vomit') and whether this is something a poem should be dealing with. Pupils could also pick up on very straightforward, almost modern style of description ('bonnet'). Pupils do not have to present both sides of the argument.

'Eden Rock'

LEVEL 2

Question	Type and structure	Answer possibilities
1 How can you tell that the poet is recalling a memory?	**Thought** 6 marks – 3 PEELs Per PEEL, 1 mark for point and evidence, 1 mark for explanation	• use and repetition of word 'same' suggests timelessness or recall of a picture: immobility of scene, as nothing ever changes, has photographic quality of a memory. • age of parents is 'twenty-five' and 'twenty-three': the narrator gives the impression of being a grown man, which would make it impossible that his parents are that young, suggesting a memory. • terrier 'still two years old': this sounds as though dog has not aged, which is impossible, except in memories. • clothing of parents: dress 'Drawn at the waist' and 'tweed suit' are old-fashioned styles of dress: suggest scene takes place a long time ago. • picnic on 'stiff white cloth' (as opposed to car rug): nowadays a picnic is an informal affair, while a white cloth suggests a special occasion, suggesting the scene happened a while ago.
2 Explain the significance of line 13	**Thought** 4 marks – 2 PEELs Per PEEL, 1 mark for point and evidence, 1 mark for explanation	• 'The sky whitens' suggests light comes closer or becoming stronger: represents approach of death/purging/salvation, as in near-death situations. • 'The sky whitens' could also suggest memory fading, like a photo exposed to too much light. • 'three suns' suggests three centres of gravity, three important beings: these could be the souls of mother, father and narrator; could also refer to the Holy Trinity which is the goal of the souls. • 'lit': as death (darkness) approaches, the souls (the dead) shine through and light the way forward or light up the sky.
3 What does the river represent in the poem?	**Thought** 6 marks – 3 PEELs Per PEEL, 1 mark for point and evidence, 1 mark for explanation	• a boundary of some sort, because they call from the 'other bank': this suggests there are two definite sides and crossing is perceived as hard. • 'stream-path' suggests that there is a way along the river, which could be life (walking along the river of life); the dead are on other side. • 'Crossing is not as hard as you might think' – the river could be the river of death (Styx, Acheron) which separates the land of the living from the land of the dead; crossing would be perceived as difficult as you have to die and observe certain rituals (like possibly and classically pay the ferryman). • 'They beckon' suggests river that has to be crossed to reach a promised land/paradise. • Have to immerse yourself in a river 'over the drifted stream' could also suggest a river of baptism (Jordan) that leads to new life.

English for Common Entrance Answer Book

Question	Type and structure	Answer possibilities
4 What is the last line referring to?	**Thought** 6 marks – 3 PEELs Per PEEL, 1 mark for point and evidence, 1 mark for explanation	• dying: 'crossing is not as hard as you might think' – crossing the boundary between life and death is usually seen as traumatic experience, but here it seems a lazy, comfortable event. • paradise: the title 'Eden Rock' and the fact the parents are forever young ('twenty-three' and 'twenty-five') – image of heaven is not a bright scene with angels, but a very down-to-earth image. • seeing his parents again: picnic scene (e.g. 'sprigged dress') shows they are just very straightforward, almost simple, people and he did not think they would be so conventional. • did not think his parents (or dying) would be so familiar, homely (picnic and parents, skimming stone) – when thinking about seeing loved ones again, we tend to imagine great emotional scenes, but this is very relaxed.
5 What does the title 'Eden Rock' suggest?	**Thought (simplified)** 3 marks – 1 mark per point made	• Eden is Biblical paradise so suggests a better world • rock is a fixed place/anchor in the earth • suggests a lighthouse • sounds like a real place the poet has actually visited • Eden rock could be demarcation point (boundary rock) between earth and paradise

LEVEL 1

Question	Type and structure	Answer possibilities
1 What does the word 'Eden' make you think of?	**Thought** 2 marks – depending on detail of answer, award 1 or 2 marks	Eden is the name of the garden in which Adam and Eve first lived; it is the name for (earthly) Paradise.
2(a) Three quotations that tell you that time has stood still	**Thought (split)** **Evidence** 2 marks – 1 mark per appropriate quotation	• repetition of word 'same' • age of parents 'twenty-five' and 'twenty-three' • terrier 'still two years old' • 'sprigged dress / Drawn at the waist' and 'tweed suit' • picnic on 'stiff white cloth'
2(b) Explain your choices in detail	**Explanation** 6 marks – 2 marks per explanation; simple explanation will get 1 mark	(In the same order as the quotations above.) • use and repetition of word 'same' suggests that nothing has changed, which would be true of a picture or a memory. • the narrator sounds like a grown man. His parents can only be 23 and 25 if he is recalling them at some earlier time. • this sounds as though the dog has not aged, which is impossible, except in memories. • the clothing of parents sounds old-fashioned, which suggests the scene takes place a long time ago. • the fact that the parents do not use a car rug, but seem to make the picnic quite a special event, suggests a long time ago.
3 What is going on in lines 13–16?	**Recall** 4 marks – 1 mark per point mentioned	• the sky grows brighter, almost painfully light • he has the feeling that there are three sources of light in the sky • the mother protects her eyes from the glare • the mother looks at the narrator • the mother is on the other side of a stream • the father spins a stone along the surface of the river
4(a) Two quotations about crossing	**Thought (split)** **Evidence** 2 marks – 1 mark per appropriate quotation	• 'they beckon to me' • 'see where the stream-path is' • 'crossing is not as hard' • 'I had not thought it would be like this'
4(b) Explain your choices in detail	**Explanation** 4 marks – 2 marks per explanation; simple explanation will get 1 mark	(In the same order as the quotations above.) • crossing is not something you would do of your own free will, so you need encouragement. • the parents point out where there's a way through the river that makes crossing easy, which suggests that all ways across are equally easy. • people would expect the crossing to be hard, but it isn't, as the parents, who have already crossed, say. • narrator is surprised at how easy the crossing is.
5 What is the poem really about?	**Thought** 6 marks – 2 PEELs Per PEEL, 1 mark for point and evidence, 1 mark for explanation	• about dying: 'crossing is not as hard as you might think' – we think of dying (crossing) as being hard, but the poem says it is like the memory of a picnic. • about how memories affect you: 'I had not thought it would be like this' – poem shows how memories change through time. • how you will never see your parents as they really are: 'father, twenty-five' – the most we will know of our parents are a few memories or photographs.

'A Boy in Church'

LEVEL 2

Question	Type and structure	Answer possibilities
1 What is happening inside and outside of the church?	**Recall** 2 marks – 1 mark per point made Both inside and outside must be mentioned for full marks	Inside: • people are praying • vicar is holding a sermon • people are singing hymns • a boy is bored • a boy is staring at his surroundings and outside Outside: • it is raining • it is windy • trees are swaying (in the wind)
2 How can you tell boy is bored?	**Thought** 6 marks – 3 PEELs Per PEEL, 1 mark for point and evidence, 1 mark for explanation	• he is not listening: 'gabble-gabble' or 'tuneful babble' – the boy cannot make out what the vicar is saying, it is all a blur to him, suggesting he is letting his mind drift, which is a sign of boredom. • he is detached from his surroundings: 'Not knowing nor much caring' – he has no clue what is going on around him and is not bothered either, suggesting it bores him. • he is more interested in what is going on outside: 'to catch better' – he shifts position so he can see what is going on outside, hinting that what is going on inside is of no interest to him. • he does pointless maths: 'add the hymns up over and over' – he is occupying his mind with sums that serve no purpose; this is not something a boy would normally do, so he must be very bored, especially as he does it repeatedly. • he looks at his surroundings: 'Who's that Saint by the Lake?' – he is absorbed in details that are of no real importance to him, meaning his mind is searching for things to do.
3 How does rhyme add to the effect of the poem?	**Technique** 4 marks – 2 PEELs Per PEEL, 1 mark for point and evidence, 1 mark for explanation	• rhyme scheme is regular: ABABCC – the regularity of the rhyme underlines the predictability and boredom of the situation. • cross rhyme in first four lines: ABAB – is slightly more 'muddled' form of rhyme scheme, mirroring the confusion outside. • cross-rhyme in first four lines: ABAB – interlinks the lines, suggesting the 'Prayer-chains' the people are praying in the poem. • rhyming couplet at end: CC – brings each stanza to a calm close, suggesting either boredom or that there is a force that calms (like prayer).

Question	Type and structure	Answer possibilities
4 How does the poet bring the scene outside to life?	**Technique** 6 marks – 3 PEELs Per PEEL, 1 mark for point and evidence, 1 mark for explanation	• repetition: 'wetter and wetter' – suggests that rain is very strong and emphasises how everything is soaked, even the plants. • alliteration: 'tossing trees' – short sharp 't' sound mirrors the jerky movements of the trees and twigs (that possibly tap on the church wall). • metaphor: 'tortured copse' – tortured means making someone experience great pain; here the strength of the wind makes the trees writhe as though they are suffering greatly. • simile: 'like a shadow-show' – in a shadow-show there is no sound just black on white and exaggerated movements; this suggests the trees are silhouetted against the sky and moving a lot, almost overdoing the swaying. • metaphor: 'dumb blast' – dumb means unable to speak; although the wind is strong, the boy cannot hear it howling, as he is inside; this gives the scene a slightly eerie touch, as we do not experience the scene as we would expect. • simile: 'like madmen praying' – madmen tend to exaggerate, move in too obvious ways; the fact that the trees seem to be praying like madmen suggest they are at the mercy of the wind and don't want to be; they are being beaten about frantically.
5(a) What do the last two lines suggest?	**Thought** 1 mark – 1 point to be made	That there is some similarity between the trees and the congregation, as both are praying
5(b) In what ways are the trees, people praying and the boy linked?	**Thought** 6 marks – 3 PEELs Per PEEL, 1 mark for point and evidence, 1 mark for explanation	• Trees are linked to congregation as they are 'like madmen praying' – the trees are being beaten about and are having difficulties, much like people when they turn to prayer. The fact that both are compared to 'madmen' suggests either that praying is futile and they are therefore mad, or that they are praying frantically. • boy linked to trees: 'shift my elbows' – he is observing the trees initially out of boredom, but then he starts thinking about them, how they are buffeted about by the wind; the boy's observation of the trees leads him to thoughts about the congregation and praying. • boy linked to congregation: 'ugly, serious people' – boy cannot empathise with the act of prayer and finds it boring; however, it seems to affect him nevertheless as he thinks about the people praying and finds comfort in the church. • congregation linked to trees: 'they never bend or sway or lurch' – although this is said of the church, this suggests the same is true of the congregation: they are not subject to the same whims of nature and can pray in more peace; the church is a bulwark against the elements (literally and metaphorically).

LEVEL 1

Question	Type and structure	Answer possibilities
1(a) What is happening inside the church?	**Recall** 2 marks – 1 mark per point made	• people are praying • vicar is holding a sermon • people are singing hymns • a boy is bored • a boy is staring at his surroundings and outside
1(b) What is happening outside?	**Recall** 2 marks – 1 mark per point made	• it is raining • it is windy • trees are swaying (in the wind)
2(a) Two quotes that show the boy is bored	**Thought (split)** **Evidence** 2 marks – 1 mark per appropriate quotation	• 'gabble-gabble' or 'tuneful babble' • 'Not knowing nor much caring' • 'to catch better/The full round sweep of heathered hill' • 'add the hymns up over and over' • 'Who's that Saint by the Lake?'
2(b) Explain your choices in detail	**Explanation** 4 marks – 2 marks per explanation; simple explanation will get 1 mark	(In the same order as the quotations above.) • he is not listening, as he does not understand what the vicar is saying; it is all a blur to him. • he has no clue what is going on around him and is not bothered either, suggesting it bores him. • he shifts position to see outside better, meaning he is more interested in trees than what is going on in the church. • he occupies his mind with sums that serve no purpose, suggesting he is trying to find something worthwhile to do. • he looks at the detail of his surroundings, meaning his mind is searching for things to do.
3(a) Rhyme scheme	**Technique (split)** **Evidence** 3 marks – 1 mark per point mentioned	• last two lines rhyme (rhyming couplet) • lines one and three rhyme (cross rhyme) • lines two and four rhyme (cross rhyme) • rhyme scheme is ABABCC • sometimes in the rhyme the last syllable is not stressed (e.g. brasses, swaying)
3(b) Effect of the rhyme	**Explanation** 2 marks – 2 marks for detailed explanation; simple explanation will get 1 mark	• rhyme scheme is regular and predictable, which mirrors the boy's boredom: in church everything is the same and monotonous, like the rhyme. • the cross rhyme is slightly dynamic like the trees swaying to and fro.

Question	Type and structure	Answer possibilities
4 How does the poet make the description of outside effective?	**Technique** 2 + 4 marks – 2 PEELs Per PEEL, 1 mark for point and evidence, 2 marks for explanation, depending on detail	• repetition: 'wetter and wetter' – suggests that rain is very strong and emphasises how everything is soaked, even the plants. • alliteration: 'tossing trees' – the alliteration makes the image of trees swaying to and fro more memorable. • metaphor: 'tortured copse' – tortured means making someone experience great pain; here the strength of the wind makes the trees writhe as though they are suffering greatly. • simile: 'like a shadow-show' – in a shadow-show there is no sound just black on white; this suggests the trees are silhouetted against the sky and moving without a sound, making the scene strange. • metaphor: 'dumb blast' – dumb means unable to speak; although the wind is strong, the boy cannot hear it howling, as he is inside. • simile: 'like madmen praying' – madmen tend to exaggerate, move in too obvious ways; the fact that the trees seem to be praying like madmen suggests they are being beaten about heavily.
5 In what way are the trees and the praying people similar?	**Thought** 4 marks – 2 PEELs Per PEEL, 1 mark for point and evidence, 1 mark for explanation	• in the last two lines the trees are compared to 'madmen praying' – the people in the church are praying too, so the trees are similar. The people do not move much, but the trees do: possibly inside the people are very agitated as one generally is when turning to pray. • the church is stable and does not 'bend or sway or lurch', which suggests the people praying are more protected than the trees. • the trees are called 'madmen' and this reflects on the people praying; the fact that both are compared to 'madmen' suggests either that praying is pointless and they are therefore mad to pray or to believe praying will make a difference, or that they are praying frantically.

Mark scheme for Prose for a purpose

(Paper 1, Section B, Questions 1–3)

Mark	Descriptors
1–11	Not relevant to the chosen task; clarity weak owing to poor organisation and technical inaccuracy; very short and undeveloped with little attention to detail.
12–15	Generally relevant to the task; ideas clearly communicated and organised into paragraphs; some attention to detail; style and tone generally appropriate for the chosen task; spelling sufficiently accurate.
16–19	Mainly relevant to the task; ideas clearly communicated and well structured in an effective and interesting way; good attention to detail; style and tone adapted well for the chosen task; spelling generally accurate; a good range of vocabulary and expression.
20–25	Consistently relevant to the task; ideas developed fully and well-structured in an original and stylish way; excellent attention to detail; essay much enhanced by style and tone; spelling consistently accurate; a wide range of vocabulary and expression.

Mark scheme for Writing about books

(Paper 1, Section B, Question 4)

Mark	Descriptors
1–11	Knowledge and understanding of the text(s) not relevant to the task; clarity weak owing to poor organisation and technical inaccuracy; very short and undeveloped.
12–15	Knowledge and understanding of the text(s) generally relevant to the task; some reference to the text made to support ideas; ideas clearly communicated and organised into paragraphs; spelling sufficiently accurate.
16–19	Knowledge and understanding of the text(s) mainly relevant to the task; good reference to the text to develop ideas; ideas clearly communicated; well-structured essay; spelling generally accurate.
20–25	Knowledge and understanding of the text(s) consistently relevant to the task; sound insight shown; close reference to the text to develop ideas fully; ideas clearly communicated; detailed and well-structured essay; spelling generally accurate; a good range of appropriate vocabulary.

Mark scheme for Creative writing

(Paper 2, Section B)

Mark	Descriptors
1–11	Not relevant to the chosen task; clarity weak owing to poor organisation and technical inaccuracy; very short and undeveloped with little attention to detail.
12–15	Generally relevant to the task; ideas clearly communicated and organised into paragraphs; some attention to detail; style and tone generally appropriate for the chosen task; spelling sufficiently accurate.
16–19	Mainly relevant to the task; ideas clearly communicated and well structured in an effective and interesting way; good attention to detail; style and tone adapted well for the chosen task; spelling generally accurate; a good range of vocabulary and expression.
20–25	Consistently relevant to the task; ideas developed fully and well-structured in an original and stylish way; excellent attention to detail; essay much enhanced by style and tone; spelling consistently accurate; a wide range of vocabulary and expression.

Explanation of descriptors

Relevance to task

This checks whether the essay is answering the question.

Paper 1: Are the points dealing with the topic? Does the evidence being used relate to the title? It is important that you do not go off track, but keep your essay focused on the title at all times.

Paper 2: Make sure, if re-interpreting the title, that it is clear you are still writing to task.

Structure

Your essay should have a clear introduction, main part and conclusion. These parts should not only be visible and recognisable, but should also fulfil their function well. Within the main part, your essay should also be structured so that individual points flow one to the next and are easily picked out.

Use paragraphs to make the structure visible. If your writing needs a special layout (like a letter) then make sure you are applying this in the exam.

Your essay should be long enough that you have dealt with the topic in sufficient detail and length that your line of argument is clear.

Technical accuracy

To gain high marks it is vital that your basics of grammar are correct. Capital letters and full stops are an absolute minimum, but apostrophes, commas and speech marks should also be used correctly.

Spelling

Much like technical accuracy, your basic spelling should be accurate. You should not misspell common words. Where you are unsure of a spelling, it should be recognisable from what you wrote which word you meant.

Words in the exam paper should not be misspelt.

Clarity

Paper 1: Make sure your points are clear and that you are writing them in a clear manner. Don't construct too long sentences in which either you or the reader get lost. Plan your conclusion so that your arguments build up to it.

Paper 2: Don't get caught up in your plot; stick to your plan to make your story as clear as possible.

Vocabulary

Use words that fit what you are saying. If you are trying to argue a complex point that requires a lot of thought, it will not impress if you use very simple language. The more precise your choice of words, the better.

Reference to text

This applies only when writing about a book.

You should use the scenes to develop your argument. Bear in mind therefore that the scenes are there to support what you have to say and not the main thing. Make sure your choice of scenes fits the title and your purpose. Don't simply retell the story; mention only as much of the scenes as you need to make your point.

Attention to detail/development of ideas

How well do you know what you are writing about?

Paper 1: You should provide in-depth points or arguments that show you have a good understanding of the main issues at stake. This means that you should not necessarily go with the first ideas that come into your head, but use the planning time to think of what lies at the core of each topic.

For example, a discussion about school uniform is not mainly about looks or comfort, but about individuality and conformity.

Paper 2: Use literary techniques to bring your story to life and focus on detail when describing the outside world as well as thoughts and emotions. For example, use:

- Powerful and unusual words – no slang!
- Precise verbs
- Adjectives and adverbs
- Sensory language
- Images (similes and metaphors)
- Alliteration, assonance and onomatopoeia

BUT don't overdo it!

Style and tone

Paper 1: Make sure you write in a formal tone of voice. Avoid colloquial language. The techniques you use and the way you write should fit the genre you are writing in.

Paper 2: Use a variety of sentence openers and connectives and vary your sentence length (use simple, compound and complex sentences).

Practice paper 1

Bringing the Cows In

LEVEL 2

Question	Type and structure	Answer possibilities
1 Why does Herriot throw himself down on the ground?	**Thought** 4 marks – 2 PEELs Per PEEL, 1 mark for point and evidence, 1 mark for explanation	• he is exasperated about his lateness: 'I was an hour behind time already' – he has a full day ahead of him and the current job is taking him longer than it should, making him stressed and tense as he still doesn't know when this job will end. • he is ready to give up: 'disbelief' – they have spent over an hour trying to get the cows in with no success and now the farmer says he'll get someone who can imitate a fly to help. This sounds ridiculous and Herriot can't see how that could be helpful, so he is ready to throw the towel in. • he is anxious about the other farmers waiting: 'the long succession of farmers … cursing me heartily' – as a vet you are dependent on what clients think of you. If Herriot is always spectacularly late then he will get a bad reputation, which will not help him with his job. He is powerless to do anything about this, though, so he throws himself on the ground in his anxiety.
2 Describe the first appearance of Sam Broadbent	**Recall** 4 marks – 1 mark per point made Must be in own words	(In words from text.) • large • fat • riding slowly on very small bicycle • heels on pedals, feet and knees sticking out at right angles • tufts of greasy black hair • skull cap like an old bowler without the brim • unshaven • vacant and incurious eyes

Question	Type and structure	Answer possibilities
3 How does Herriot make Sam's humming effective?	**Technique** 6 marks – 3 PEELs Per PEEL, 1 mark for point and evidence, 1 mark for explanation	• describing detail 'cheeks worked as though he was getting everything into place' – the fact that he has to prepare his face builds tension as this suggests the humming is not a simple sound to produce and requires careful preparation. The detail stops time, so to speak, and the reader is left expectant as to what will happen next. • sibilance: 'sudden swelling of angry sound, a vicious' – the harsh 's' sound (mainly) at the beginning of these words is a strong and angry hiss that mirrors the dangerous buzzing of the flies. As we tend to emphasise the beginning of words more, the 's' has even more effect. • onomatopoeia: 'humming' – the low 'u' sound combined with the 'mm' sound mirror a dull vibration. This is like the flies 'warming up' or approaching from far away. The hum is not threatening yet, as it is more low-pitched, but it suggests something dangerous is approaching. • onomatopoeia: 'buzzing' – the vibrating 'zz' sound combined with the 'i' sound following it gives a higher-pitched sound that sounds like the movement of many wings; the 'zz' sound is slightly aggressive and suggests insects swarming angrily. • onomatopoeia: 'zooming' – the 'z' sound at the beginning is harder because emphasised and mirrors the sound of insect wings beating. The 'oom' sounds like something passing at speed, suggesting the insect is flying towards you. • emotional response: 'in alarm' – if you are alarmed you are worried about something and fear that something bad will happen. If the author reacts with alarm to a sound then it must be quite a dangerous sound. • hyperbole: 'for the kill' – insect bites or stings very rarely kill, but saying that the insects are coming in 'for the kill', as though they could end someone's life, makes them (their noise) sound more dangerous. • short sentences: 'The effect on the heifers was electric.' – The short sentence at the beginning of the paragraph emphasises that the cows react sharply. 'Electric' means to do with power and this can shock, meaning the cows were stunned as though they were hit by high voltage. The short suddenness of the sentence reflects the sudden reaction of the cattle. • metaphor: 'frightened block' – a block is a solid, indistinguishable mass. Although the cows are not really a block, the word suggests they are packed very closely together in fright, as none of them wants to expose herself to the angry flies.

Question	Type and structure	Answer possibilities
4 Find and explain three humorous quotations	**Technique** 6 marks – 3 PEELs Per PEEL, 1 mark for point and evidence, 1 mark for explanation	• repetition: 'Did you say imitate a fly?' – Herriot repeats what the farmer has just said in disbelief as he does not think the farmer can be serious. The farmer answers normally, showing he thinks what he has said is perfectly natural. The contrast between Herriot's disbelief and the farmer's deadpan straightforwardness is humorous. • contrast: 'large, fat man … very small bicycle' – the fact that Sam comes on a bicycle that is obviously too small for him is comic, as it is ridiculous that a grown man should be riding a children's bike without realising he looks silly. The fact that his knees stick out add to the incongruity of the situation. • personification: 'They had obviously enjoyed every minute of the morning's entertainment' – by pretending the cows are human beings who have obviously found what has happened so far a fun game, he makes the frustration of them not doing what he wants more marked, as it suggests they *could* do what he wants them to. This is funny, as cows do not behave like humans and are not doing what they are for any real reason: they are just cows. Making them seem more is funny. • short descriptions: 'He was clearly a one-pace man' – such a pithy description, reducing a man to a short description, is humorous as it is not what we would expect. Also, the description suggests he does not move like normal people. In the situation we would expect him to walk briskly up the hill, but he can only walk one way; the contrast between the urgency of the situation and his slowness is also humorous.
5 What kind of person is Sam?	**Thought** 5 marks – 2 PEELs Per PEEL, 1 mark for point and evidence, 1 mark for explanation; 1 extra mark for quality and depth of response	• calm: 'ascended the slope unhurriedly' – although Herriot and Kay are panicking slightly, trying to keep the herd together, Sam is not worried and walks slowly, showing he is calm. • sure of himself: 'fixed the animals' – the fact he did not run up the hill shows he feels confident that he can bring the cows in, no matter what. Staring at them before blowing again suggests he is in control of the situation and the cows. • helpful: 'Sam's come to give us a hand' – although it is probable that Sam does not have a lot to do, he nevertheless helps out when he's needed. which is not obvious, suggesting he is helpful. • simple: 'vacant and incurious' – if eyes stare blankly it means there is not a lot of thought going on in the head behind them, so we have the impression Sam is simple. Also he does not talk at all throughout the passage, also suggesting he is simple. • unkempt: 'tufts of greasy black hair stuck out at random' – even if a farmer, people would usually take a bit more care about their appearance; that Sam doesn't suggests he does not find it important and prefers to go around looking like a scarecrow.

LEVEL 1

Question	Type and structure	Answer possibilities
1 Two reasons why Herriot throws himself on the ground	**Recall** 4 marks – 2 marks per point made, depending on detail	• he does not believe what he has just been told, that a person who can imitate a fly can help get unwilling cows into a shed. • he is frustrated that he has already spent one hour trying to get cows in and has still not been successful and so he is running late. • he is upset that he is making a bad impression on all the farmers waiting for his arrival as he obviously has a tight schedule, which the farmers would expect him to keep.
2 Describe Sam in your own words as much as possible	**Recall** 5 marks – 1 mark per point made up to 4 marks 1 extra mark if own words	(In words from text) • large • fat • greasy black hair • tufts stick out at random from under a cap • wears a skull cap • rides a bicycle that is too small for him (with heels on pedals, feet and knees sticking out at right angles) • unshaven • vacant and incurious eyes
3(a) Two quotations that bring Sam's humming to life	**Technique (split)** **Evidence** 2 marks – 1 mark per appropriate quotation	• 'sudden swelling of angry sound, a vicious' • 'humming' • 'buzzing' • 'zooming' • 'in alarm' • 'for the kill' • 'The effect on the heifers was electric.'

Question	Type and structure	Answer possibilities
3(b) Explain your choices in detail	**Explanation** 4 marks – 2 marks per explanation; simple explanation will get 1 mark	(In the same order as the quotations above.) • the repeated 's' sounds (sibilance) are harsh as they are at the beginning of these words. This mirrors the strong and angry hiss of the flies. • the onomatopoeia of the low 'u' sound with the 'mm' sounds like a dull vibration. This is like the flies 'warming up' or approaching from far away. It suggests something dangerous is approaching. • the onomatopoeia of the vibrating 'zz' sound is higher-pitched and sounds like the movement of many wings; the 'zz' sound is aggressive and suggests insects swarming angrily. • the 'z' sound at the beginning is harder and mirrors the sound of an insect flying. The 'oom' sounds like something passing at speed, suggesting the insect is flying quickly towards you. • if you are alarmed you are worried about something and fear that something bad will happen. If the author reacts with alarm to a sound then it must be quite a dangerous sound. • insect bites or stings very rarely kill, but exaggerating that the insects are coming in 'for the kill', as though they could end someone's life, makes them (their noise) sound more dangerous. • The short sentence at the beginning of the paragraph emphasises that the cows react suddenly. 'Electric' means to do with power and this can shock, meaning the cows are stunned, are in shock.
4(a) Three quotations that are funny	**Technique (split)** **Evidence** 3 marks – 1 mark per appropriate quotation	• 'Did you say imitate a fly?' • 'large, fat man … very small bicycle' • 'They had obviously enjoyed every minute of the morning's entertainment' • 'He was clearly a one-pace man'
4(b) Explain your choices	**Explanation** 3 marks – 1 mark per brief explanation	(In the same order as the quotations above.) • Herriot repeats what the farmer has just said because he can't believe that sounding like a fly can help. This is funny as the farmer is serious. • the fact that Sam is huge and the bicycle is small is ridiculous (and what clowns often do too), as the two don't fit together in any way. • by pretending the cows are human beings who have obviously found what has happened so far a fun game, he makes the frustration of them not doing what he wants more funny. • reducing a man to a short description, is humorous as it is not what we would expect and there must be more to him than just that.
5 What kind of a person is Sam?	**Thought (simplified)** 4 marks – 2 Points with Evidence Per PE, 1 mark for point and 1 mark for evidence	• calm: 'ascended the slope unhurriedly' • sure of himself: 'fixed the animals' • helpful: 'Sam's come to give us a hand' • simple: 'vacant and incurious' • does care about his appearance: 'tufts of greasy black hair stuck out at random'

English for Common Entrance Answer Book

'Death of a Gardener'

LEVEL 2

Question	Type and structure	Answer possibilities
1 What does the gardener do during winter?	**Recall** 2 marks – 1 mark per point made	• rests • watches the rain • sleeps • smokes his pipe • dreams beside the fire
2 What do we learn about the winter?	**Thought** 6 marks – 3 PEELs Per PEEL, 1 mark for point and evidence, 1 mark for explanation	• time when gardener is thankful: 'grateful for the slow/ Nights' – during the spring and summer he has a lot of work and the days are long, meaning he can do more; in winter the nights are long and not filled with work. • time when work s easy: 'undemanding days' – if the days do not demand much from him it means that the work he has to do is easy, so winter is a time of ease. • snow covers all making work impossible: 'thatching the roof again / With silence' – if snow covers roof, it must be covering everything else; that it covers all with silence suggests there is no life underneath and thus no gardening to do. • time to dream and relax: 'spark/Hissed from his pipe and he dreamed' – in winter the gardener has time to smoke a pipe and dream, which is not something he would usually be able to do; gives a cosy impression of winter. • Winter seems never-ending: 'the pause grew big with cold' – winter is a pause in life as all seems dead and if it grows big it feels like that is all there is and it will never end; the cold underlines the fact that winter is a time of lifelessness and stasis.
3 How does the poet make the seasons come to life?	**Technique** 6 marks – 3 PEELs Per PEEL, 1 mark for point and evidence, 1 mark for explanation Both seasons must be mentioned for full marks	Winter • describing detail: 'snow/Padding the window' – padding is a thick protective layer that is soft; so the snow is like insulation, blanketing the windows, almost protecting them. • metaphor: 'thatching the roof …/With silence' – the thatch protects the house suggesting that the snow is covering the house like a protective layer that hushes all inside, like a blanket. • sibilance: 'Mice in the shed scuffled like leaves' – the repetition of the soft 's' sound emphasises how all is quiet as the only sound that can be heard is a soft 's', which is almost no sound at all. Spring • metaphor: 'light sharpened' – sharper means more damaging, brighter, suggesting the light is clearer and more powerful now; the sun is no longer glowing gently, but is shining vigorously with new life and possibly painfully. • metaphor: 'earth drew breath' – when you draw breath you are born or come to life; the earth after the 'death' of winter is now coming to life again; it is being reborn. • simile: 'like a child in the womb' – the earth is like a child about to be born, the soil is full of seeds waiting to be born; this is like the kicks of a baby that is ready to be born; so spring is when the earth is ready to be born (again).

Question	Type and structure	Answer possibilities
4 What makes it clear that the gardener is getting old?	**Thought** 6 marks – 3 PEELs Per PEEL, 1 mark for point and evidence, 1 mark for explanation	• work is getting hard: 'troubled him' – if bringing out the barrow and spade is difficult, then this means the man must be getting old. • he can no longer work as quickly: 'slower' – if he is not as fast as he used to be this could suggest that he is aging and no longer has the muscles to work quickly. • he has to interrupt his work frequently: 'Long intervals' – if he has to pause for a long time in his work this tells us he no longer has the stamina to work continuously, suggesting he is old. • his work lacks vigour: 'hesitant blade' – if he is unsure where to put the blade or has to dither to put the spade in the right place he is obviously shaky, which suggests age. • he can no longer move smoothly: 'Hands tremulous' – while there are a number of reasons why hands can become shaky, here they are obviously wobbling due to age as there is no other discernible cause and the gardener dies soon after.
5 Was the gardener's death an easy one?	**Response** 5 marks – according to quality of response 1–2: simple response that shows little reference to the poem and little thought 3–4: good, solid response with some reference to the poem and some coherent points, with examples 5: sophisticated piece using elements from the poem and points backed up with examples throughout	Answers will vary. Reference could be made to the nature of the gardener's death (gentle, died in his sleep), the fact that he died while doing his work (which can be interpreted as either good or bad), that he was growing old, irony of him dying in spring when the earth is being (re)born. Pupils do not have to present both sides of the argument.

LEVEL 1

Question	Type and structure	Answer possibilities
1(a) Three things the gardener does in winter	**Recall** 3 marks – 1 mark per point made	• rests • watches the rain • sleeps • smokes his pipe • dreams beside the fire
1(b) Two things the gardener does in spring	**Recall** 2 marks – 1 mark per point made	• he 'wakes' (starts work again) • stands on the grass • fetches spade and wheelbarrow
2 What do we learn about the winter	**Thought** 4 marks – 2 PEELs Per PEEL, 1 mark for point and evidence, 1 mark for (brief) explanation	• time when work is easy: 'undemanding days' – if the days do not demand much from him it means that the work he has to do is easy, so winter is a time when there is little work to do. • snow covers all making work impossible: 'thatching the roof again/ With silence' If snow covers roof, it must be covering everything else, which means you can't really do much work in the garden. • time to dream and relax: 'he dreamed' – in winter the gardener has time to dream, which means he has lots of time; this also makes the winter feel snug and cosy. • winter seems never-ending: 'the pause grew big' – winter is a pause in life as all seems dead and if it grows big it feels like that is all there is and it will never end.
3(a) Two examples of onomatopoeia from the first stanza	**Technique (split)** **Evidence** 2 marks – 1 mark per onomatopoeic word	• padding • scuffled • hissed
3(b) Explain how the words make the description of winter vivid	**Explanation** 4 marks – 2 marks per explanation; simple explanation will get 1 mark	(In the same order as the quotations above.) • padding suggests something soft that will protect, which is like the snow that covers everything. • scuffled is a quick, quiet movement, like the mice are trying to reach a safe place, suggesting all want to be home in winter and if they move, then it is quickly and quietly. • when a spark lights up it glows brightly for a moment and makes a soft sound, which shows it has caught flame, so here the pipe is on, helping the gardener relax.
4(a) Two quotations that show the gardener is old	**Thought (split)** **Evidence** 2 marks – 1 mark per appropriate quotation	• slower • long intervals • hesitant blade • hands tremulous

Question	Type and structure	Answer possibilities
4(b) Explain your choices	**Explanation** 4 marks – 2 marks for detailed explanation; simple explanation will get 1 mark	(In the same order as the quotations above.) • he can no longer work quickly meaning he is not as fast as he used to be, which suggests he has grown old. • he has to interrupt his work frequently, which means he is no longer strong enough to work for a long time without interruption. • he is unsure where to put the blade or has to dither to put the spade in the right place, which means he is obviously shaky. • he can no longer move smoothly; shaky hands are a classic sign of age.
5 What tells you that the gardener's death was an easy one?	**Thought** 4 marks – 2 PEELs Per PEEL, 1 mark for point and evidence, 1 mark for (brief) explanation	• his death is like the earth is keeping a promise made to him: earth keeps 'faith with him' – if you keep faith with someone, it means you stand by them, so here the earth (garden) is with the gardener as he dies, making it a good death. • the earth (garden) makes sure she gets the gardener: 'claimed him' – the gardener was obviously important to the earth and so she makes sure she gets him. As a garden is (usually) a beautiful place, this is positive. • he dies peacefully: 'as he slept' – dying in your sleep is the easiest and least painful way to die. • he does not die alone: 'beside his guardian spade' – the spade is almost like a guardian angel, suggesting the gardener does not really die lonely.

Practice paper 2

Barn Dance

LEVEL 2

Question	Type and structure	Answer possibilities
1 How have the people decorated the grange	**Recall** 4 marks – 1 mark per point made	• string of electric bulbs • bulbs covered with painted paper • floor swept • orchestra stage of grainpallets • bandshell from sheeting • lights in fruitcans at base of stage
2 How does the author bring the barn dance to life?	**Technique** 8 marks – 4 PEELs Per PEEL, 1 mark for point and evidence, 1 mark for explanation	• repetition: 'watched' – the fact that the word is repeated suggests that a lot of the goings-on at the dance are people watching other people. This could be because they are resting or shy or trying to find out what kind of people are there. The repetition emphasises this aspect of the dance. • sensory language: 'The air smelled of straw and sweat and a rich spice of colognes' – by focusing on these three smells, the main elements of the dance are highlighted (which is supported by the sibilance): barn, people exerting themselves and people trying to win favour with others. • sibilance: 'struggled … slammed … stepped' – the three verbs used to describe the accordion player are sibilant, bringing them closer together. This makes the description more lively as the alliteration brings rhythm to the sentence, mirroring the rhythm of the playing. • onomatopoeia: slammed' – the harsh 'sl' sound at the beginning is like a slide or slap that then has a dull, blunt impact with the 'mm-ed' sound that mirrors something quite soft banging into something. • contrast: 'separate and collective paths' – this suggests that the dance has an overall order as all paths are together, held together by the rhythm of the music and yet all are different, as each pair dances differently. The contrast shows how the dance happens all at the same time and yet is different for each pair.
3(a) Describe the ritual the boys perform before entering	**Recall** 2 marks – 1 mark per point made	• pass around a bottle of mescal • lick salt from their hands after drinking • take chewing gum
3(b) Why do they do this?	**Thought (simplified)** 1 mark – 1 mark per appropriate idea	• they hope alcohol will give them courage • they want to bond before the dance, to underline they are a group • the chewing gum is so their breath smells fresh and not of alcohol

Question	Type and structure	Answer possibilities
4 Comment on the sentence structure	**Technique** 4 marks – 2 PEELs Per PEEL, 1 mark for point and evidence, 1 mark for explanation	• a lot of long sentences joined with 'and' • this long stringing together of phrases is mainly used to describe surroundings and works like a person taking in detail in stages (e.g. lines 1–4 or 9–11). • long sentences also push action forward and suggest a natural and almost inescapable progression from one thing to the next (e.g. lines 19–21 or 27–29). • sudden short sentences. • usually emphasise some important action (e.g. 'When she turned again she smiled'). Embedded in the longer sentences, these short sentences stand out, so their message becomes more important. • they can also signify more time passing (e.g. 'They drank'). Here the single sentence suggests more time passing and thus a pause in the story.
5 What can you infer about the relationship between Grady and the girl?	**Thought** 6 marks – 3 PEELs Per PEEL, 1 mark for point and evidence, 1 mark for explanation	• Grady is interested in her: 'she wore a blue dress and her mouth was red' – that these are described (the last two paragraphs are from Grady's pov) show that Grady is interested in her looks, suggesting he is at least interested in her. • He is infatuated by her: 'the nape of her neck pale as porcelain' – he is obviously observing her closely, suggesting he thinks her beautiful, but is also attracted to her as you only notice such fine detail if you have an interest in the person. • She has been looking out for Grady: 'Her eyes … swept across him' – she sees Grady and looks at him. When dancing you should look at your partner, but she is looking at Grady, which suggests she is more interested in him than her partner. • She likes Grady: 'she smiled' – you smile at people you like; here she is smiling at Grady while dancing with someone else, which suggests she likes Grady a lot, as she is making a point of making him see her affection for him. • She is attracted to Grady: 'put her face against his shoulder' – putting your cheek against someone else's shoulder is a very intimate movement that shows she trusts Grady and is attracted to him and is willing to show this.

LEVEL 1

Question	Type and structure	Answer possibilities
1 How had the grange been prepared for the barn dance?	**Recall** 4 marks – 1 mark per point made	• string of electric bulbs • bulbs covered with painted paper • floor swept • orchestra stage of grainpallets • bandshell from sheeting • lights in fruitcans at base of stage
2(a) Three quotations that bring the barn dance to life	**Technique (split)** **Evidence** 3 marks – 1 mark per appropriate quotation	• 'watched … watched' • 'The air smelled of straw and sweat and a rich spice of colognes' • 'struggled … slammed … stepped' • 'slammed' • 'separate and collective paths'
2(b) Explain your choices in detail	**Explanation** 6 marks – 2 marks per explanation; simple explanation will get 1 mark	(In the same order as the quotations above.) • the fact that the word 'watched' is repeated suggests that a lot of people are just watching other people. This could be because they are resting or shy or trying to find out what kind of people are there. • by focusing on these three smells, the main elements of the dance are highlighted: that it's in a barn (straw), that people are dancing hard (sweat) and that people are trying to impress each other (cologne). • the three verbs used to describe the accordion player are sibilant, bringing them closer together. The alliteration brings rhythm to the sentence, mirroring the rhythm of the playing. • the onomatopoeia here rests on the harsh 'sl' sound at the beginning which is like a slide or slap that then has a dull, blunt impact with the 'mm-ed' sound that mirrors something quite soft banging into something. • the contrasting adjectives show how the dance has an overall order as all dances are in time to the rhythm of the music and yet all are different, as each pair dances differently.
3(a) What do the boys do before entering the barn?	**Recall** 2 marks – 1 mark per point made	• pass around a bottle of mescal • lick salt from their hands after drinking • take chewing gum
3(b) Why do they do this?	**Thought (simplified)** 2 marks – 2 marks for any appropriate idea	• they hope alcohol will give them courage • they want to bond before the dance, to underline they are a group • the chewing gum is so their breath smells fresh and not of alcohol
4 Why has author used long and short sentences the way he has?	**Technique (simplified)** 2 marks – 2 marks for any appropriate idea	• long sentences for description • long sentences push action forward • short sentences emphasise what they contain • short sentences are like a pause

Question	Type and structure	Answer possibilities
5(a) Three quotations that tell you Grady and the girl are interested in each other	**Thought (split)** **Evidence** 3 marks – 1 mark per appropriate quotation	• 'she wore a blue dress and her mouth was red' • 'the nape of her neck pale as porcelain' • 'Her eyes … swept across him' • 'she smiled' • 'put her face against his shoulder'
5(b) Explain your choices briefly	**Explanation** 3 marks – 1 mark per brief explanation	(In the same order as the quotations above.) • the fact that Grady notices these details suggests he is interested in her. • he is observing her closely, suggesting he thinks her beautiful, but is also attracted to her. • while dancing with someone else she looks at Grady, which suggests she is interested in him. • she is smiling at Grady while dancing with someone else, which suggests she likes Grady a lot. • putting your cheek against someone else's shoulder is a very intimate movement that shows she is attracted to Grady.

'Legs'

LEVEL 2

Question	Type and structure	Answer possibilities
1 First three kinds of legs that Scannell mentions	**Recall** 3 marks – 1 mark per point made	• babies • schoolboys • schoolgirls (the schoolboys' sisters)
2 How is the description of the legs effective?	**Technique** 8 marks – 4 PEELs Per PEEL, 1 mark for point and evidence, 1 mark for explanation	• simile: 'as soft / As dough or mashed potato' – dough is white and pliable and mashed potato is squishy and soft; both suggest that the legs of the baby have no bones in them, but are soft and malleable. • consonance: 'scabs and starred with scars' – in describing schoolboys' legs with wounds on them, Scannell uses words that repeat sc and r. Both are harsh sounds that remind of the freshly healed wounds sustained by boys. • metaphor: 'cruelly blotched' – the marks on old or ugly legs are not crue , as they are a product of age, not of someone taking pleasure in inflicting them; pretending they are makes us pity the people with such legs. • metaphor: 'muscled double weapons' – in describing legs in army boots he refers to legs as weapons, so as instruments that are harmful, which they are, in a way, because they carry a soldier; also, the quads resemble gun barrels. • simile: 'long and smooth as milk' – milk is a white and silky drink, suggesting the legs are pale and smooth; the long reminds us of milk being poured. As we tend to associate milk with children, these are possibly children's legs. • simile: 'like marble badly stained' – marble is a white stone that often has coloured veins of black or dark blue in it. In this way it is similar in colour to legs; if the marble is badly stained, it suggests the veins are more blotches.
3 Explain what the poet is telling us about the two types of legs	**Thought** 4 marks – 2 PEELs Per PEEL, 1 mark for point and evidence, 1 mark for explanation	• babies' legs are shapeless: 'creamy bonelessness' – when you look at a baby's legs you have no idea what kind of legs they will be; they seem to lack structure and solidity, being just white putty. • young girls' legs are thin, without contours: 'possess/ No calves as yet' – when young girls have only stick-like legs with no curves to them, but when they do gain shape, they become attractive. • even unsightly legs are interesting: 'the veined and cruelly blotched' – even legs that are horrible or ugly to look at because they are marked or strangely shaped are interesting, if only because they are also called legs, although they are so different from beautiful ones. • legs become like their owners' occupation: 'muscled double weapons' – when soldiers march their muscles bunch and are hard and seem to be weapons, suggesting the legs somehow assimilate their owners' jobs.

Question	Type and structure	Answer possibilities
4 How do rhythm and rhyme make the poem effective?	**Technique** 6 marks – 3 PEELs Per PEEL, 1 mark for point and evidence, 1 mark for explanation Both rhythm and rhyme must be mentioned for full marks	Rhyme • a lot of internal rhymes: 'veined … stained' (lines 18 and 19) – the fact that the poet has also rhymed inside lines increases the poem's pace and also makes it hold together more as there are more links between lines. • rhyme scheme starts out seemingly regular (ABABCDD), but then this disintegrates. Irregularity and partial regularity of the rhymes mirrors the different kinds of legs: most are regular, but some aren't. • most of the lines rhyme at least once with one other line in the poem, which gives the poem sense of all the lines belonging together. Also, most rhymes therefore come in pairs, like legs. Rhythm • mainly regular rhythm (iambic pentameter) – this is a steady rhythm that is similar to walking, which is what legs mainly do. • regular rhythm leads to lines of same (stress) length, like legs, although there are occasional differences, like some legs are longer and some shorter.
5 Meaning of the last three lines	**Response** 4 marks – according to quality of response 1: simple response that shows little reference to the poem and little thought 2–3: good, solid response with some reference to the poem and some coherent points, with examples 4: sophisticated piece using elements from the poem and points backed up with examples throughout	Answers will vary. Reference could be made on how strange that all these different phenomena are called 'legs', how they please and have brought the poet pleasure (by their looks as well as by him writing about them). Top pupils will refer to the literal and metaphorical meaning of 'transport' (the joke underlined by the feminine rhyme).

English for Common Entrance Answer Book

LEVEL 1

Question	Type and structure	Answer possibilities
1 To whom do the first two legs belong?	**Recall** 4 marks – 2 marks per point made	• babies • schoolboys
2(a) Two similes from the poem	**Technique (split)** **Evidence** 2 marks – 1 mark per simile	• 'as soft / As dough or mashed potato' • 'Like fine twin creatures of rare pedigree' • 'like marble badly stained' • 'long and smooth as milk'
2(b) Explain their effectiveness in detail	**Explanation** 4 marks – 2 marks per explanation; simple explanation will get 1 mark	(In the same order as the quotations above.) • dough is white and mushy and mashed potato is squishy and soft; both suggest that the legs of the baby have no bones in them. • rare pedigree means having a family tree that is uncommon; the legs are being compared to expensive pets who are bred for their excellent qualities. • marble is a white stone that often has coloured veins of black or dark blue in it. In this way it is similar in colour to legs; if the marble is badly stained, it suggests the veins are not little rivers, but huge blotches. • milk is a white and silky drink, suggesting the legs are pale and smooth; the long reminds us of milk being poured.
3 Explain in your own words what the poet is saying with the three leg descriptions	**Recall** 6 marks – 2 marks per description written in own words	• babies: when you look at a baby's legs you have no idea what kind of legs they will be; they seem to lack bones and are just a squishy mess. • young girls: their legs are thin and stick-like, without curves, but when they do gain shape, they become attractive. • unsightly legs: even legs that are horrible or ugly to look at because they are marked or strangely shaped are interesting, as they are also a type of leg. • soldiers: the legs are like the people who have them, so a soldier's legs are like weapons as he marches: hard and dangerous, because they are muscular. • Scotsmen: the legs of various nationalities reflect what the people mainly eat, so a Scotsman's legs have knees like porridge, which they hide in their kilts.
4(a) How does regular rhythm contribute to the poem's effectiveness?	**Technique (simplified)** 2 marks – 2 marks for any appropriate explanation	• a steady rhythm is similar to walking, which is what legs mainly do. • regular rhythm leads to lines of same (stress) length, like legs, which come in pairs of the same length.
4(b) How do rhymes bring the poem to life?	**Technique (simplified)** 2 marks – 2 marks for any appropriate explanation	• internal rhymes: 'veined … stained' (lines 18 and 19) makes the poem faster to read and also links the lines more closely together. • the partly irregular and partly regular rhyme scheme is similar to different types of legs: most are regular, but some aren't. • most of the lines rhyme at least once with one other lines in the poem, which gives the poem a sense of all the lines belonging together. Also, most rhymes therefore come in pairs, like legs.

Question	Type and structure	Answer possibilities
5 What does the poet mean with the last three lines?	**Response** 5 marks – according to quality of response 1–2: simple response that shows little reference to the poem and little thought 3–4: good, solid response with some reference to the poem and examples 5: engaging answer using elements from the poem and points backed up with examples throughout	Answers will vary. Reference could be made on how strange that all these different phenomena are called 'legs', how they please and have brought the poet pleasure (by their looks as well as by him writing about them). Top answers will refer to the literal and metaphorical meaning of 'transport' (the joke underlined by the feminine rhyme).

Practice paper 3

Vienna

LEVEL 2

Question	Type and structure	Answer possibilities
1 What does Bryson not like about European trains?	**Recall** 4 marks – 1 mark per point made	• they are tediously slow • division of the carriages into compartments is antiquated • being in the compartment is like being locked in a waiting-room • there is no privacy in the compartments • you are forced to talk to or at least deal with strangers • being trapped with other people makes you think about your body
2 How does the author bring his visit to the cathedral to life?	**Technique** 6 marks – 3 PEELs Per PEEL, 1 mark for point and evidence, 1 mark for explanation	• simple description: 'very grand' – grand is something that is meant to impress and that is built in a generous way. By limiting himself to just this word, he gives a general impression of the cathedral being a magnificent building. • emotional response: 'cold shiver' – if you are in an uncanny place you will feel a cold shiver: you react to the sense of being abandoned; considering that the church is meant to be a place of comfort, this reaction shows how cold the interior is. • tricolon: 'the brass … the pews … the marble' – by naming the three different materials that are predominant in every church, Bryson achieves the effect that you think the whole church is drab. • use of atmospheric adjectives: 'dull … worn … heavy' – although these are all simple words, they are all linked to decay and ageing, thus suggesting that the cathedral has not been looked after, but left to rot. • atmospheric descriptions: 'lifeless' and 'dead' – the repetition of a word associated with death when describing the church suggests it is just a husk, a skeleton with no life inside. • simile: 'as if all the natural luminescence had been drained from it' – light is something positive that makes a place seem alive; if light is drained this is like energy disappearing due to some outside force; both these words show the cathedral has faded and is dark and dull; the 'drained' even suggests it drains the energy of its visitors.
3(a) What does Bryson not like about Viennese cafés?	**Recall** 3 marks – 1 mark per point made	• they are just restaurants • they have no charm • they are not full of eccentric characters • the coffee is not sensational • service is slow • waiters are always unfriendly

Question	Type and structure	Answer possibilities
3(b) What does Bryson like about the Hawelka?	**Recall** 3 marks – 1 mark per point made	• it is dark • it is dishevelled and musty (suggesting it has character) • it is friendly • he is served coffee without asking for it • it has lots of newspapers: old and new
4 How does the author make the USA Today episode funny?	**Technique** 4 marks – 2 PEELs Per PEEL, 1 mark for point and evidence, 1 mark for explanation	• hyperbole: 'Put these on the fire' – the waiter is trying to be kind and giving the author what he thinks he'd like to read, but the author's exaggerated response is in stark contrast to this helpfulness, making it funny. • use of dialogue: '"No, no," I protested' – the noting down of the actual words makes the scene come to life and helps the reader imagine how the author is trying to stop the waiter, which is humorous, as the waiter is doing the exact opposite of what Bryson is saying. • irony: 'other great thinkers of our age' – Sylvester Stallone is an actor famous for his muscles, but not for his mind. Bryson would like to read something intellectually challenging but is stuck with Stallone, and the irony highlights his discontent and also makes it funny through contrast. • witty repartee: 'these are for lining drawers' – the waiter is giving him reading material, but Bryson says the magazines can only be used for storage. The contrast between the waiter's purpose and Bryson's attitude makes for humour.
5 Based on the extract, would you like to visit Vienna?	**Response** 5 marks – according to quality of response 1–2: simple response that shows little reference to the passage and little thought 3–4: good, solid response with some reference to the passage and examples 5: engaging answer using elements from the passage and points backed up with examples throughout	Answers will vary. Reference could be made to the descriptions of café and cathedral, which are both uninviting; pupils might question Bryson's judgement or want to see for themselves if it really is that bad. More able pupils might pick up on the fact that Bryson all in all obviously liked Vienna (line 11), so there must be more to the city than just what is in the extract.

LEVEL 1

Question	Type and structure	Answer possibilities
1 What does Bryson not like about European trains?	**Recall** 4 marks – 1 mark per point made	• they are tediously slow • division of the carriages into compartments is antiquated • being in the compartment is like being locked in a waiting-room • there is no privacy in the compartments • you are forced to talk to or at least deal with strangers • being trapped with other people makes you think about your body
2(a) Two quotations that bring his visit to the cathedral to life	**Technique (split)** **Evidence** 2 marks – 1 mark per appropriate quotation	• 'very grand' • 'cold shiver' • 'dull … worn … heavy' • 'lifeless' and 'dead' • 'as if all the natural luminescence had been drained from it'
2(b) Explain your choices in detail	**Explanation** 4 marks – 2 marks per explanation; simple explanation will get 1 mark	(In the same order as the quotations above.) • grand is something that is meant to impress. By limiting himself to this word, he gives a general impression of the cathedral being a magnificent building. • if you are in an uncanny place you will feel a cold shiver: you react to the sense of being abandoned; considering that the church is meant to be a place of comfort, this reaction shows how cold the interior is. • although these are all simple words, they are all linked to decay and ageing, thus suggesting that the cathedral has not been looked after. • the repetition of a word associated with death when describing the church suggests it is just a husk, a skeleton with no life inside. • light is something positive that makes a place seem alive; if light is drained this is like energy disappearing due to some outside force; both these words show the cathedral has faded and is dark and dull.
3(a) What does Bryson not like about Viennese cafés?	**Recall** 3 marks – 1 mark per point made	• they are just restaurants • they have no charm • they are not full of eccentric characters • the coffee is not sensational • service is slow • waiters are always unfriendly
3(b) What does he like about the Hawelka?	**Recall** 3 marks – 1 mark per point made	• it is dark • it is dishevelled and musty (suggesting it has character) • it is friendly • he is served coffee without asking for it • it has lots of newspapers: old and new

Question	Type and structure	Answer possibilities
4 Two humorous quotes from lines 28–34 with brief explanation	**Technique (simplified)** 2 + 2 marks – 1 mark per appropriate quotation and 1 mark per brief explanation	• 'Put these on the fire' – the waiter is trying to be kind and the author just says throw it away. The contrast between the two intentions is humorous. • 'other great thinkers of our age' – Sylvester Stallone is an actor famous for his muscles, but not for his mind, so pretending he is a thinker is funny. • 'these are for lining drawers' – the waiter is giving him reading material, but Bryson says the magazines can only be used for storage. The contrast between the waiter's purpose and Bryson's attitude makes for humour.
5 Would you like to visit Vienna?	**Response** 5 marks – according to quality of response 1–2: simple response that shows little reference to the passage and little thought 3–4: good, solid response with some reference to the passage and examples 5: engaging answer using elements from the passage and points backed up with examples throughout	Answers will vary. Reference could be made to the descriptions of café and cathedral, which are both uninviting; pupils might question Bryson's judgement or want to see for themselves if it really is that bad. Some pupils might pick up on the fact that Bryson all in all obviously liked Vienna (line 11), so there must be more to the city than just what is in the extract.

'Goatsucker'

LEVEL 2

Question	Type and structure	Answer possibilities
1(a) What do the goatherds accuse the Goatsucker of doing?	**Recall** 2 marks – 1 mark per point made	• milking their goats dry • fly noisily through the night
1(b) What does it actually do?	**Recall** 2 marks – 1 mark per point made	• chases cockchafers • follows luna moths
2 How does the poet make the Goatsucker seem hellish?	**Technique** 8 marks – 4 PEELs Per PEEL, 1 mark for point and evidence, 1 mark for explanation	• onomatopoeia: 'burring' – the 'b' is quite a hard sound and that combined with the 'urr' suggests a noisy flight or a menacing buzz, like from a demon or evil flying beast. • word creations: 'vampiring' – a vampire is a blood-sucking undead and a creature of evil. By saying the Goatsucker is vampiring it suggests the bird is not only a bloodsucker, but is also evil. • alliteration: 'claw-cuts' – the hard and sudden 'k' sounds mirror someone or something scratching heftily at something. The fact that it is a claw sounds demonic, as demons have claws. • use of names: 'Devil-bird' – the Devil is of course the ruler of hell and purely evil. By using this other name for the Goatsucker, Plath is suggesting the Goatsucker is a pet or a special bird of the devil. • metaphor: 'chip of ruby fire' – a chip is a small sliver of material; by saying the eye of the Goatsucker is a thin piece of glowing red, Plath is making it sound demonic, as demons have fiery red eyes. • metaphor: 'wings of witch cloth' – witches are reputed to fly invisibly through the night on magic broomsticks; this metaphor suggests that like witches, the Goatsucker travels through the night air by magic; as witches are evil, the bird is as well.
3 How do the goatherds and dairy farmers react to the Goatsucker?	**Thought** 4 marks – 2 PEELs Per PEEL, 1 mark for point and evidence, 1 mark for explanation	• they only hear it: 'they hear/The warning whirr' – although the people only hear the bird, they interpret the sound of its flight as a warning and immediately assume, because it flies by night, that it is evil. • the dairy farmer imagines his cows fall sick: 'Dreams that his fattest cattle dwindle' – the farmer has never seen the bird claw his cattle and it is not even certain his herd is suffering: he dreams it all. This shows how strong superstition is, making the farmer believe things with no evidence.

Question	Type and structure	Answer possibilities
4 How does Plath create an atmosphere of darkness?	**Technique** 4 marks – 2 PEELs Per PEEL, 1 mark for point and evidence, 1 mark for explanation	• repetition: 'Moon full, moon dark' – the moon rules the night, so the repetition emphasises that it is night time; the word 'dark' reinforces this mood. • powerful language: 'dwindle, fevered' – dwindle is to become less and less and fevered is to run a temperature due to sickness; both of these words suggest illness and fading away, both actions that key into an atmosphere of darkness. • metaphor: 'ebony air' – ebony is a type of wood that is black. Suggesting the night is impenetrable, solid black, adds to the atmosphere. • powerful language 'shadows' – to shadow is to follow someone as though you weren't there. Even when describing the harmless pursuits of the Gcatsucker, Plath uses a word that is related to night, as shadows are also the dark where there is no sun.
5 What is the Goatsucker really?	**Thought** 5 marks – 1 mark for answer and 4 marks for 2 PEELs as support Per PEEL, 1 mark for point and evidence, 1 mark for explanation	Goatsucker is another name for the nightjar, a nocturnal bird that feeds on insects. Answers may vary, but pupils should realise it is a flying, nocturnal insectivore (so bat is equally possible). • nocturnal: 'wakes with darkness and till dawn works hard' – if the creature gets up with dark, it means it is awake through the night, meaning it is nocturnal. • flying creature: 'bird', 'Devil-bird' or 'wings of witch cloth' or 'fly-by-night' – all these suggest the Goatsucker has wings of some sort or is at least similar to a bird as it flies freely. • insectivore: 'shadows only … / Cockchafers and the wan, green luna moth' – both of these are night-flying insects and are the prey of the Goatsucker, as the 'shadows' suggests. • it has a large mouth surrounded by tactile hair or whiskers: 'cave-mouth bristle beset' – a cave is a large cavity, so the mouth is large; bristles are long, thick hairs, so its mouth has bristles around it.

LEVEL 1

Question	Type and structure	Answer possibilities
1(a) What do the farmers accuse the Goatsucker of doing?	**Recall** 2 marks – 1 mark per point made	• milking their goats dry • cutting into their cows
1(b) What does it actually do?	**Recall** 2 marks – 1 mark per point made	• chases cockchafers • follows luna moths
2(a) Three quotations that make the Goatsucker seem devilish	**Technique (split)** **Evidence** 3 marks – 1 mark per appropriate quotation	• 'burring' • 'vampiring' • 'claw-cuts' • 'Devil-bird' • 'chip of ruby fire' • 'wings of witch cloth'
2(b) Explain your choices in detail	**Explanation** 6 marks – 2 marks per explanation; simple explanation will get 1 mark	(In the same order as the quotations above.) • the 'b' is quite a hard sound and the 'urr' suggests noisy flight; the whole creature buzzes menacingly like a demon or evil flying beast. • a vampire is a blood-sucking creature of evil. This suggests the bird is not only a bloodsucker, but is also evil. • the hard and sudden 'k' sounds mirror someone or something scratching heftily at something. The fact that it is a claw sounds demonic. • the Devil is of course the ruler of hell and purely evil. The name suggests the Goatsucker is a pet or a special bird of the devil. • a chip is a small sliver of material; if the eye of the Goatsucker is a thin piece of glowing red, this is like a demon's fiery red eyes. • witches are said to fly invisibly through the night on magic broomsticks; so the Goatsucker travels through the night air by magic like evil witches.
3 Describe what the goatherds and the dairy farmers are doing in the poem	**Recall** 4 marks – 2 marks per description	• goatherds are listening to the whirr and burring of the Goatsucker • dairy farmers are dreaming that their best cows are being slashed by the Goatsucker, making them ill and thin
4 Three quotations that contribute to the dark atmosphere	**Recall** 3 marks – 1 mark for each appropriate quotation	• 'Moon full, moon dark' • 'dwindle' • 'fevered' • 'ebony air' • 'shadows' • 'cave-mouth'

Question	Type and structure	Answer possibilities
5 What do you think the Goatsucker is?	**Thought** 5 marks – 1 mark for answer and 4 marks for 2 PEELs as support Per PEEL, 1 mark for point and evidence, 1 mark for brief explanation	Goatsucker is another name for the nightjar, a nocturnal bird that feeds on insects. Answers may vary, but pupils should realise it is a flying, nocturnal insectivore (so bat is equally possible). • nocturnal: 'wakes with darkness and till dawn works hard' – if the creature gets up with dark, it means it is awake through the night, meaning it is nocturnal. • flying creature: 'bird', 'Devil-bird' or 'wings of witch cloth' or 'fly-by-night' – all these suggest the Goatsucker has wings of some sort or is at least similar to a bird as it flies freely. • insectivore: 'shadows only … / Cockchafers and the wan, green luna moth' – both of these are night-flying insects and are the prey of the Goatsucker, as the word 'shadows' suggests. • it has a large mouth: 'cave-mouth' – a cave is a large cavity, so the mouth is large.

Practice paper 4

Too Soft

LEVEL 2

Question	Type and structure	Answer possibilities
1(a) What is Baba's view of what real men should do?	**Recall** 3 marks – 1 mark per point made	• go hunting • not read poetry • not write poetry • play soccer
1(b) In what way does Amir not conform?	**Recall** 1 mark – 1 mark for any appropriate point	• he reads books • he reads poetry
2 How does the author make attempts at either playing or supporting football vivid?	**Technique** 4 marks – 2 PEELs Per PEEL, 1 mark for point and evidence, 1 mark for explanation Pupils must analyse either playing or supporting, NOT both	Playing • onomatopoeia: 'blundering' – the heavy 'b' and 'd' sounds are reminiscent of little hits, like someone bumping into things; paired with the dull 'un' and 'er' sounds the word gives the impression of someone off-balance and heavy. • sibilance: 'shambled about … on scraggy legs' – the 's' and 'sh' sounds in this phrase suggest sliding, rather like the action of shambling, a walk that is dragging the feet slowly. • powerful adjective: 'scraggy legs' – scraggy means thin and without muscles; legs that are thin and bony are not athletic and will have difficulties playing a sport involving a lot of legwork, like football. • use of dialogue: 'I'm open! I'm open!' – use of direct speech brings life, especially in this exclamation that, with its repetition and use of the exclamation mark, shows the narrator's desperation to be noticed and to join in. Using the actual words makes the scene more direct. Supporting • rhetorical question: 'Certainly I could manage that, couldn't I?' – by asking this question, the narrator is making it appear a simple task; the 'certainly' underlines this. This makes the reader agree with the narrator and think it will be easy. • onomatopoeia: 'yelped' – the round 'y' and 'l' sounds combined with the high 'e' is like someone opening their mouth to bring out high-pitched, short sounds; that the narrator makes such sounds like a dog shows his aggression. • simple description: 'faked interest' – faking is pretending something is real when it isn't; in this case Amir pretends he is interested in football when he isn't. The clear description shows that for Amir it was a simple decision to deceive. • onomatopoeia: 'cheered' – the long 'ee' sound in the middle of the word is like a smile or a high-pitched sound, both mirroring the joy and noise of cheering; Amir is trying to be enthusiastic as he supports the team.

Question	Type and structure	Answer possibilities
3 How does the author bring the Buzkashi tournament to life?	**Technique** 6 marks – 3 PEELs Per PEEL, 1 mark for point and evidence, 1 mark for explanation	• alliteration: 'midst of a melee' – the 'm' sound is not clear and its repetition suggests the mix-up that is in a melee. Also, the alliteration emphasises the powerful word 'melee' for a confused crowd. • list: 'kick, claw, whip, punch' – various forms of hurting a person are listed and the fact that they are listed with no final 'and' suggests they are happening quickly; the list suggests that there are many of these, showing how brutal the tournament is. • onomatopoeia: 'bellowed' – the open and sonorous 'ow' sound is like a mouth wide open, to shout loudly and the explosive 'b' at the beginning suggests the cry is sudden. • alliteration: 'yipping and yelling' – the repetition of the 'y' sound emphasises the high-pitched nature of the sounds, the whoops of triumph, of these two onomatopoeic words. The 'y' sound is a short, quick opening, like brief cries of excitement. • onomatopoeia: 'clatter' – the hard 'kl' sound at the beginning is the hoof striking the ground and the following 't' and 'r' sound like the repercussion of the initial strike, making the word mirror the sound of a horse galloping.
4 What is the relationship between Amir and Baba like?	**Thought** 6 marks – 3 PEELs Per PEEL, 1 mark for point and evidence, 1 mark for explanation Pupils must explain both Amir's and Baba's side for full marks	• Amir wants to please Baba: 'faked interest as long as possible' – although he is obviously not interested in soccer, Amir pretends to the best of his ability that he likes it. He only does this to please his father. • he is hurt by his father's indifference: 'I escaped my father's aloofness' – his father seems to be a far-away figure with whom he has no real relationship. The fact that he needs to get away from this coldness suggests that he is hurt by it. • sees the positive in Baba: 'valiant efforts to conceal the disgusted look' – rather than focus on the rejection of Baba, the narrator describes how he tries to hide his disgust; 'valiantly' suggests a struggle and bravery, suggesting he sees the positive in Baba. • Baba is angry at Amir's softness: 'Baba's hands clenched' – when someone clenches his hand it is a sign of aggression, as he is making a fist. Baba is driving back from the tournament, while Amir is crying, showing he is soft-hearted, which angers Baba. • determined to make Amir a real man: 'Baba wouldn't give up' – when Amir is no good at football, he doesn't accept that, but tries to interest him in another manly pursuit.
5 Who do you sympathise with more?	**Response** 5 marks – according to quality of response 1–2: simple response that shows little reference to the text and little thought 3–4: good, solid response with some reference to the text and examples 5: sophisticated answer using elements from the text and points backed up with examples throughout	Answers will vary. For Amir reference could be made to the fact that he tries hard to please his father and reacts quite naturally to a brutal death. For Baba reference could be made that he is trying to prepare his son for a world he knows is harsh and also that he tries to hide his emotions.

LEVEL 1

Question	Type and structure	Answer possibilities
1(a) What is Baba's view of real men?	**Recall** 3 marks – 1 mark per point made	• go hunting • not read poetry • not write poetry • play soccer
1(b) In what way does Amir not conform?	**Recall** 1 mark – 1 mark for any appropriate point	• he reads books • he reads poetry
2(a) Two quotations that show Amir is not good at football	**Technique (split)** **Evidence** 2 marks – 1 mark per appropriate quotation	• 'blundering' • 'shambled about … on scraggy legs' • 'scraggy legs' • '"I'm open! I'm open!"'
2(b) Explain your choices briefly	**Explanation** 2 marks – 1 mark per simple explanation	(In the same order as the quotations above.) • the word sounds like someone clumsily bumping into things. • this phrase sounds like someone dragging their feet slowly. • legs that are thin and bony are not athletic and will have difficulties playing football. • the narrator is desperate to be noticed and to join in, but the others ignore him because he's bad.
3(a) Two quotations that make the tournament come to life	**Technique (split)** **Evidence** 2 marks – 1 mark per appropriate quotation	• 'midst of a melee' • 'kick, claw, whip, punch' • 'bellowed' • 'yipping and yelling' • 'clatter'
3(b) Explain your choice in detail	**Explanation** 4 marks – 2 marks per explanation; simple explanation will get 1 mark	(In the same order as the quotations above.) • the 'm' sound is not a clear sound and its repetition suggests the mix-up that is in a melee. Also, the alliteration emphasises the powerful word 'melee' for a confused crowd. • various forms of hurting a person are listed which suggests they are happening quickly; the list also suggests that there are many of these, showing how brutal the tournament is. • the open and deep 'ow' sound is like a mouth wide open, to shout loudly and the explosive 'b' at the beginning suggests the cry s sudden. • the repetition of the 'y' sound emphasises the high-pitched nature of the sounds. The 'y' sound is a short, quick opening, like brief cries of excitement. • the hard 'kl' sound at the beginning is the hoof striking the ground and the following 't' and 'r' sound the following beats, making the word mirror the sound of a horse galloping.

Question	Type and structure	Answer possibilities
4(a) Find and explain a quotation of how Amir sees Baba	**Thought** 1+2 marks – 1 mark for quotation and 2 marks for explanation; simple explanation will get 1 mark	• Amir wants to please Baba: 'faked interest as long as possible' – although he is obviously not interested in soccer, Amir pretends to the best of his ability that he likes it. He only does this to please his father. • his father doesn't care about him: 'I escaped my father's aloofness' – his father seems to be a far-away figure with whom he has no real relationship. The fact that he needs to get away from this coldness suggests that he is hurt by it. • sees that Baba is trying not to be unfriend y to him: 'valiant efforts to conceal the disgusted look' – rather than focus on Baba's anger, the narrator describes how he tries to hide his disgust; 'valiantly' suggest a struggle and bravery, showing he sees the positive in Baba.
4(b) Find and explain a quotation of how Baba sees Amir	**Thought** 1+2 marks – 1 mark for quotation and 2 marks for explanation; simple explanation will get 1 mark	• he is angry at Amir's softness: 'Baba's hands clenched' – when someone clenches his hand it is a sign of aggression, as he is making a fist. Baba is driving back from the tournament, while Amir is crying, showing he is soft-hearted, which angers Baba. • determined to make Amir a real man: 'Baba wouldn't give up' – when Amir is no good at football, he doesn't accept that, but tries to interest him in another manly pursuit.
5 Who do you sympathise with more?	**Response** 5 marks – according to quality of response 1–2: simple response that shows little reference to the text and little thought 3–4: good, solid response with some reference to the text and examples 5: engaging answer using elements from the text and points backed up with examples throughout	Answers will vary. For Amir reference could be made to the fact that he tries hard to please his father and reacts quite naturally to a brutal death. For Baba reference could be made that he is trying to prepare his son for a world he knows is harsh and also that he tries to hide his emotions.

LEVEL 2

Question	Type and structure	Answer possibilities
1 Retell Jack's story in your own words	**Recall** 4 marks – 1 mark per point made	• Jack, a black boy, is left by his mother when three weeks old • he is hidden under a stone and left to die • some white people hear his crying • they take him in and make him part of the family • he lives a happy life with the white people • he dies an old man
2 Why is there no punctuation or capitals?	**Thought (simplified)** 3 marks – 1 – 2 marks per explanation depending on detail	• makes it sound more primeval, more natural, as no sophistication of punctuation • makes story flow more, as no stops • makes it more like a story to be told rather than written down
3 How does the poet bring her story to life?	**Technique** 6 marks – 3 PEELs Per PEEL, 1 mark for point and evidence, 1 mark for explanation	• simile: 'curled like a grub' – a grub is a larval state of a beetle that has no real legs and is just a pale, curled body that lives in the earth. The comparison suggests the child is not fully grown and is helpless, its limbs being of no use. • simile: 'hard as bone' – bone is the last thing left of you when you die and also a symbol of death. The simile suggests that the veldt is a place of death, with no mercy. • ambiguity: 'ditched' – ditched is a colloquial term for throwing away or leaving behind; ditch is also a little channel by the side of the road where people often leave things, suggesting the baby was ditched in a ditch. • metaphor: 'gave the slip to death' – when you give someone the slip, you manage to escape from them. Although the baby is helpless, it still manages to fool death and not die. The metaphor is a cliché, but the unusual word order makes it fresher. • onomatopoeia: 'moan' – the soft, humming 'm' sound at the beginning followed by the open, loud 'oa' mirrors someone in distress trembling and then crying out.

Question	Type and structure	Answer possibilities
4 Comment on the rhythm, rhyme and stanza structure	**Technique** 6 marks – 3 PEELs Per PEEL, 1 mark for point and evidence, 1 mark for explanation Each PEEL should deal with different aspect	Rhythm • four beats per line – this is a very racy beat that rushes the poem and the story along; it is also quite a light-hearted beat, suggesting the story will be happy. • most are iambs, but lines often start with a stressed syllable – starting lines with a stress makes the rhythm stronger and more abrupt, as lines start and end on stress; makes poem more conversational, as unnecessary words cut out. Rhyme • rhyming couplets: 'stone … alone' – this is a very fast rhyme scheme that is often used in humorous poems, suggesting the poem is ultimately a happy one. • Many words and rhymes are repeated: 'stone/alone/bone/moan' – this holds the poem together even more than the rhyme scheme, as rhymes cross stanzas. With the same words used again and again the poet also creates atmosphere and a sense of inevitability. Stanzas • stanzas more or less regular four lines with rhyming couplets and each stanza tells a piece of the story; each stanza is like an episode. Pattern makes poem predictable, but also strengthens work of rhythm and rhyme. • Last line is separated: this is the ending, almost like the flourish at the end of a told story. Highlighting the line makes it clearer that this is the formulaic end.
5 Why is Jack called 'Resurrection Jack'?	**Thought** 6 marks – 3 PEELs Per PEEL, 1 mark for point and evidence, 1 mark for explanation	• he came back to life: 'Raised him up' – Jack had been left for dead and was close to dying; that he then went on to live is a sort of coming back from the dead. • he was released from his grave: 'rolled that stone' – Jesus was buried in a grave with a stone rolled in front; here Jack is being compared to Jesus, because both rose out of a tomb. • certain time spent under the stone: 'three weeks old' – although we do not know how long Jack was under the stone, Jesus spent three days in the grave and Jack's age of three weeks calls this to mind. • he starts a second life: 'that was the day when his life begun' – when you are resurrected you have an old life (Jack's first three weeks) and then a new life.

LEVEL 1

Question	Type and structure	Answer possibilities
1 Retell Jack's life	**Recall** 6 marks – 1 mark per point made	• Jack, a black boy, is left by his mother when three weeks old • he is hidden under a stone and left to die • some white people hear his crying • they take him in and make him part of the family • he lives a happy life with the white people • he dies an old man
2 Does the lack of punctuation make the poem harder or easier to read?	**Thought (simplified)** 2 marks – 1–2 marks per explanation, depending on detail	Harder • don't know where to stop • makes poem look unfamiliar and therefore more difficult Easier • don't have to worry about punctuation, freeing you up for the words • each line makes sense on its own, so don't need punctuation
3(a) Three quotations that make the story vivid	**Technique (split)** **Evidence** 3 marks – 1 mark per appropriate quotation	• 'curled like a grub' • 'hard as bone' • 'ditched' • 'gave the slip to death' • 'moan'
3(b) Explain your choices in detail	**Explanation** 6 marks – 2 marks per explanation; simple explanation will get 1 mark	(In the same order as the quotations above.) • a grub is the larva of a beetle that has no real legs and is just a pale, curled body that lives underground. The comparison suggests the buried child is not fully grown and is helpless. • bones are symbols of death. The simile suggests that the veldt is a place of death, with no mercy. • ditched is a colloquial term for throwing away or leaving behind; ditch is also a little channel by the side of the road where people often leave things, so the baby may have been ditched in a ditch. • when you give someone the slip, you manage to escape from them. Although the baby is helpless, the phrase suggests it is already clever enough to fool death. • the soft, humming 'm' sound at the beginning followed by the open, loud 'oa' mirrors someone in distress trembling and then crying out.
4(a) What does the regular rhyme scheme add to the poem?	**Technique** 2 marks – 1–2 marks per explanation, depending on detail	• it speeds up the pace of the story, making it race along and thus a more action-packed story. The fast rhymes also add a lightness to the poem. • there are not many different rhymes, which holds the poem together even more than the rhyme scheme. With the same words used again and again the poet also creates atmosphere.

Question	Type and structure	Answer possibilities
4(b) How does the strong rhythm make the poem more effective?	**Technique** 2 marks – 1–2 marks per explanation, depending on detail	• the beats are racy – not that many per line (four) – which rush the poem and the story along • lines often start with a stressed syllable, which makes the rhythm stronger and more like people talking.
5 Why is Resurrection Jack called that?	**Thought** 2 + 2 marks – 2 PEELs Per PEEL, 1 mark for point and evidence, 1 mark for explanation	• 'raised him up' – Jack had been left for dead and then lived again. • 'rolled that stone' – Jesus was buried in a grave with a stone rolled in front; Jack is being compared to Jesus, who rose from the dead. • 'that was the day when his life begun' – when you are resurrected you have an old life (Jack's first three weeks) and then a new life.

English for Common Entrance Answer Book

Practice paper 5

The Salem Witch Trials Begin

LEVEL 2

Question	Type and structure	Answer possibilities
1 What news from Salem does Elizabeth tell Proctor?	**Recall** 4 marks – 1 mark per point made	• that there's a court in Salem • that four judges from Boston have come • the Deputy Governor of the Province is heading the legal proceedings • fourteen people are in jail • the court has the power to hang • if people don't confess, they'll be hanged
2(a) What does Elizabeth say about Abby's appearance in court?	**Recall** 3 marks – 1 mark per point made	• she's acting like a saint • the crowd parts before her • she leads the other girls into court • if she screams and howls in front of someone that person is jailed for witchcraft
2(b) What does this tell you about Abigail?	**Thought (simplified)** 2 marks – either two brief explanations, or one detailed explanation	• she is charismatic, as she is obviously the leader of the girls; she is the one who leads the girls and Mary (one of the girls) looks up to her, too. • other people fear her and her power to have people jailed by just howling at them. • vengeful or power hungry, as all she has to do is scream and fall to the floor in front of someone to have them jailed; the fact that she does this rather than spare the people shows she is vengeful or power hungry.
3 Why is Proctor reluctant to go to Salem?	**Thought** 6 marks – 3 PEELs Per PEEL, 1 mark for point and evidence, 1 mark for explanation	• not sure his message will be heard: 'It is a wonder they do believe her' – he is unsure of how the mood in Salem has changed and if the people believe Abby with her stories of witchcraft, then they may not believe him when he talks reason and sense. • doesn't want to rush into anything: 'I will think on it!' – charging the main witness in a court case with fraud is a serious accusation and he does not want to do anything wrong, or else tables might turn on him and he be imprisoned. • he has no proof: 'how I may prove what she told me' – as he has no proof, it is only his word against Abigail's; while this would usually suffice, times are not normal and he is afraid his word will not count against hers. • fears Abigail may have too much influence: 'If the girl's a saint now' – if Abigail has become a saint it means she is untouchable and anybody who says anything against her could be regarded as a devil. • he still has feelings for her: 'if it were not Abigail … would you falter now?' – although this is Elizabeth talking, it is likely that Proctor does not want to act immediately against his former lover, as he might still have feelings for her. Also, he is possibly hoping he might be able to influence Abby.

Question	Type and structure	Answer possibilities
4 What is the relationship between Proctor and Elizabeth like?	**Thought** 6 marks – 3 PEELs Per PEEL, 1 mark for point and evidence, 1 mark for explanation	• he is quite harsh: '*It* is a fault' – when Elizabeth lets Mary go to Salem against Proctor's orders, he says openly that it was wrong. He does not try and say it in a kind way. • Elizabeth nags Proctor: '*quietly jeering to anger him by prodding*' – Elizabeth keeps repeating that he must go to Salem as she knows he needs to be prodded to action to do what he doesn't want to. Although not in charge, this shows she knows how to get Proctor to do what she wants. • slightly cold and distant: 'Good, then, let you think on it' – she feels let down by John and thinks he is still in love with Abigail. This makes her more cold towards him. She realises also she is not his only consideration. • he feels guilt towards Elizabeth: 'You will not judge me more' – he knows he has done wrong and regrets it, but he can't undo that. His anger at Elizabeth's prodding is due to guilt, too, as he knows what she's thinking. • Elizabeth mistrusts Proctor: 'I see what I see' – although the affair is over, Elizabeth is still suspicious and is not sure that John is absolutely loyal to her. She interprets signs unfavourably for John.
5 What is the role of the stage directions?	**Technique** 4 marks – 2 PEELs Per PEEL, 1 mark for point and evidence, 1 mark for explanation	• tell actors what to do at important moments: '*she stands and starts to walk out of the room*' – the action here is important as it highlights how she is hurt and so the stage direction is necessary to bring this across. • make the emotions clear: '*angering*' – without the stage direction, there would be a number of ways to say Proctor's speech, but the stage direction makes it clear how these words are to be spoken: that he is not resigned, but angry now. • describe the characters' thoughts: '*holding back a full condemnation of her*' – this shows that what he says is not all he thinks. The background information is important as it helps actors know what the characters truly think of one another, what they don't show in their words.

LEVEL 1

Question	Type and structure	Answer possibilities
1 What is the news Elizabeth tells Proctor?	**Recall** 4 marks – 1 mark per point made	• that there's a court in Salem • that four judges from Boston have come • the Deputy Governor of the Province is heading the legal proceedings • fourteen people are in jail • the court has the power to hang • if people don't confess, they'll be hanged
2(a) What does Elizabeth say about Abigail in court?	**Recall** 3 marks – 1 mark per point made	• she's acting like a saint • the crowd parts before her • she leads the other girls into court • if she screams and howls in front of someone that person is jailed for witchcraft
2(b) What does this tell you about Abigail?	**Thought (simplified)** 2 marks – 2 marks for any appropriate explanation	• she is the one who leads the girls and Mary (one of the girls) looks up to her, so she must be their leader and have charisma. • other people fear her and her power to have people jailed by just howling at them. • vengeful or power hungry, as all she has to do is scream and fall to the floor in front of someone to have them jailed and she does it, seemingly enjoying her power.
3(a) Two quotations that show Proctor does not want to go to Salem	**Thought (split)** **Evidence** 2 marks – 1 mark per appropriate quotation	• 'I will think on it!' • 'how I may prove what she told me' • 'If the girl's a saint now' • 'if it were not Abigail … would you falter now?'
3(b) What does each quote tell you about his reasons for not going	**Explanation** 4 marks – 2 marks per explanation; simple explanation will get 1 mark	(In the same order as the quotations above.) • accusing the main witness in a court case of lying is serious and he does not want to do anything wrong, or else tables might turn on him. • as he has no proof, it is only his word against Abigail's; while this would usually be enough, times are not normal and he is afraid his word will not count against hers. • if Abigail has become a saint it means she is untouchable and anybody who says anything against her could be regarded as a devil. He fears his influence will not be enough. • although Elizabeth says this, it is likely that Proctor does not want to act immediately against his former lover, as he might still have feelings for her.
4(a) Two quotations that show the relationship is not a happy one	**Thought (split)** **Evidence** 2 marks – 1 mark per appropriate quotation	• '*It* is a fault' • '*quietly jeering to anger him by prodding*' • 'Good, then, let you think on it' • 'You will not judge me more' • 'I see what I see'

Question	Type and structure	Answer possibilities
4(b) Explain your choices	**Explanation** 4 marks – 2 marks per explanation; simple explanation will get 1 mark	(In the same order as the quotations above.) • when Elizabeth lets Mary go to Salem against Proctor's orders, he says openly that it was wrong. He does not try to say it in a kind way, which would be more normal. • Elizabeth keeps nagging him to go to Salem and does not leave him in peace. When you prod your partner you are waiting for him or her to get angry, suggesting the relationship is strained as this is the only way she can get him to do things. • she feels let down by John and thinks he is still in love with Abigail. This makes her more cold towards him. She says these words to show she does not believe his motives, suggesting distrust. • he knows he has done wrong and regrets t, but he can't undo that. He no longer wants to be judged by Elizabeth; that she has in the past suggests their relationship is not the best. • although the affair is over, Elizabeth is still suspicious and is not sure that John is absolutely loyal to her. She does not believe what he says and interprets signs against John.
5(a) Purpose of the stage direction in line 25	**Technique (simplified)** 2 marks – 2 marks for any appropriate explanation	• to tell actors what to do at important moments – the action here is important as it shows that Proctor does not like the idea of going to Salem: as soon as she says it he reacts by turning to her; the stage direction is necessary to bring this across.
5(b) Purpose of the stage direction in line 39	**Technique (simplified)** 2 marks – 2 marks for any appropriate explanation	• makes the emotions clear – without the stage direction, there would be a number of ways Proctor could be saying this, but the stage direction makes it clear now these words are to be spoken: that he is not resigned, but angry.

'Especially When It Snows'

LEVEL 2

Question	Type and structure	Answer possibilities
1(a) Who is the poet speaking to?	**Recall** 2 marks – 1 mark per point made	• Boty • his 'darling'
1(b) Who could this be?	**Thought** 2 marks – 1 PEEL 1 mark for point and evidence, 1 mark for explanation	• obviously someone close to him: 'darling' – you usually do not call a lot of people darling, only your closest family, so Boty is probably someone from his close family (wife or daughter). • probably his wife or baby daughter: 'little Caitlin crouched to wave goodbye' – if Caitlin is a young child, then she would most naturally wave goodbye either to her mother or to a younger sibling.
2 How does the author make winter vivid?	**Technique** 6 marks – 3 PEELs Per PEEL, 1 mark for point and evidence, 1 mark for explanation	• metaphor: 'dark arms and widespread hands' – in winter the trees are stripped of their leaves and only the branches and twigs show, which are like arms and hands and because they are dark against the snow you can see them all the more clearly. • metaphor: 'angelfood' – the snow falls from heaven and it looks like crumbs of white bread, so it could be the remains of a meal from heaven; also the purity of the snow suggests it might be food for holy creatures. • metaphor: 'dark lake' – a lake is a vast expanse of water that can look dark when light reflects on it. The footprints leave marks that fill with water or that punch through to the soil, so it looks like dark lakes. • describing detail: 'tough little robins' – tough means hardened, not easily beaten; the fact that robins, usually seen as gentle birds, have to be tough shows that the winter must be hard for the birds to have to be hard. • describing detail: 'golden-spangled windows' – to spangle is to cover in bright materials, so here the windows have been covered in little bits of gold, which must be Christmas decorations.
3 Comment on the effect of repetition	**Technique** 4 marks – 2 PEELs Per PEEL, 1 mark for point and evidence, 1 mark for explanation	• sets a gloomy mood: 'dark' (lines 3 and 7) – although the poem is set in snow, the use of the word dark, twice, brings in a sad atmosphere, as it suggests that although most is bright, there is also some black. • emphasises the setting: 'especially when it snows' – this is repeated in almost every stanza and holds the poem structurally together. It is like a theme running through the poem, drawing the reader back to the setting and the question: what is especially then? • he can't get rid of thoughts: 'especially when it snows/ and keeps on snowing' – these two lines are repeated towards the end and form the last stanza. The second line suggests the snow falling does not let the poet's mind go and so he is – like the repetition – trapped to think about the thing as long as it snows.

Question	Type and structure	Answer possibilities
4 How does the poet create a mood of grief and loss?	**Technique** 6 marks – 3 PEELs Per PEEL, 1 mark for point and evidence, 1 mark for explanation	• describes the setting: 'memorial garden' – this is a place where you remember the dead (usually after they've been cremated); this setting suggests that nothing positive will happen here. • simple words: 'said goodbye' – saying goodbye is always combined with a sense of loss and thereby of sadness. When you say goodbye you often don't know when you'll see the person again. • metaphor: 'blank-eyed snow' – the eyes are said to be the mirror of the soul, so when they are blank, there is no expression and no life in them. Suggesting the snow is a lifeless, blankly gazing entity creates a sad atmosphere. • emotional appeal: 'little Caitlin crouched to wave goodbye' – mentioning a small girl saying goodbye to someone, obviously someone who has died, makes it sadder, as we can feel with the girl who possibly doesn't know what exactly is going on. • alliteration: 'dead darling' – the repeated, dull 'd' sounds have a finality about them, a closing of sound that reflects a closing of life, which reinforces a feeling of grief.
5 What happens when it snows? Give reasons	**Thought** 5 marks – 1 mark for any appropriate answer, 2 PEELs for support Per PEEL, 1 mark for point and evidence, 1 mark for explanation	• the poet remembers his dead beloved, Boty. • it started with snow: 'ever since we said goodbye' – whatever happens 'especially when it snows' started ever since Boty died, suggested by the memorial garden and the saying goodbye. As it was snowing then, snow now reminds him of her. • it has to do with death: 'his dead darling in his arms' – the final simile of the poem homes in on the figure of Lear mourning a dead beloved; this suggests that this is what the poem is about. • it must be the death of a close family member: 'little Caitlin crouched' – she would not wave goodbye to anyone who is not close family as at that age children tend not to go to funerals, unless directly involved. • the poem addresses a specific person and is dedicated to Boty – this suggests the poem was written for Boty, who must then be the person being addressed in the poem, who died. The poem is one way the poet is trying to overcome his grief.

English for Common Entrance Answer Book

LEVEL 1

Question	Type and structure	Answer possibilities
1(a) Who is Boty?	**Thought (simplified)** 2 marks – 2 marks for any appropriate idea	• obviously someone close to him as he calls her 'darling', probably his wife or daughter. • probably his dead wife or baby daughter, because Caitlin waves goodbye to her, which she'd only do to her mother or to a sibling.
1(b) Who is Caitlin?	**Thought (simplified)** 2 marks – 2 marks for any appropriate idea	• Caitlin is called 'little', so probably a child, most likely the poet's daughter. • she is either Boty's sister or Boty's daughter, as the fact that she waves goodbye at her grave suggests a close relationship.
2(a) Three quotations that make winter vivid	**Technique (split)** **Evidence** 3 marks – 1 mark per appropriate quotation	• 'dark arms and widespread hands' • 'angelfood' • 'dark lake' • 'tough little robins' • 'golden-spangled windows'
2(b) Explain your choices in detail	**Explanation** 6 marks – 2 marks per explanation; simple explanation will get 1 mark	(In the same order as the quotations above.) • in winter the trees are stripped of their leaves and only the branches and twigs show, which are like arms and hands and, because they are dark against the snow, you can see them more clearly. • the snow falls from heaven and it looks like crumbs of white bread, so it could be the remains of a meal from heaven. • 'dark lake' – a lake is a vast expanse of water that can look dark when light reflects on it. The footprints leave marks that fill with water or that punch through to the soil, so it looks like dark lakes. • tough means hardened, not easily beaten; the fact that robins, usually seen as gentle birds, have to be tough shows that the winter must be hard. • to spangle is to cover in bright materials, so here the windows have been covered in little bits of gold, which must be Christmas decorations.
3 Effect of the repetition of 'especially when it snows'	**Technique (simplified)** 2 marks – 2 marks for any appropriate answer	• this is repeated in almost every stanza and holds the poem structurally together. • it is like a theme running through the poem, drawing the reader back to the setting and the question: what is especially then? • he can't get rid of thoughts 'especially when it snows' and so he is – like the repetition – trapped to think about the thing as long as it snows.
4(a) Two quotations that show a mood of grief and loss	**Technique (split)** **Evidence** 2 marks – 1 mark per appropriate quotation	• 'memorial garden' • 'said goodbye' • 'blank-eyed snow' • 'little Caitlin crouched to wave goodbye' • 'dead darling'

Question	Type and structure	Answer possibilities
4(b) Explain your choices in detail	**Explanation** 4 marks – 2 marks per explanation; simple explanation will get 1 mark	(In the same order as the quotations above.) • this is a place where you remember the dead; this setting suggests that nothing positive will happen here. • saying goodbye is always combined with a sense of loss and thereby of sadness. When you say goodbye you often don't know when you'll see the person again. • when the eyes are blank, there is no expression and no life in them. Suggesting the snow is lifeless creates a sad atmosphere. • mentioning a small girl saying goodbye to someone, obviously someone who has died, makes it sadder, as we can feel with the girl who possibly doesn't know what exactly is going on. • the repeated, dull 'd' sounds have a finality about them, a closing of sound that reflects a closing of life.
5 What do you think happens when it snows?	**Thought** 4 marks – 2 PEELs Per PEEL, 1 mark for point and evidence, 1 mark for brief explanation	• he remembers a dead person: 'ever since we said goodbye' – whatever happens especially when it snows started ever since someone died. • it has to do with death: 'his dead darling in his arms' – the final simile of the poem suggests that this is what the poem is about. • it must be the death of a close family member 'little Caitlin crouched' – she would not wave goodbye to anyone who is not close family. • the poem addresses a specific person and is dedicated to Boty – this suggests the poem was written for Boty, who must then be the person being addressed n the poem, who died.

Although every effort has been made to ensure that website addresses are correct at time of going to press, Hodder Education cannot be held responsible for the content of any website mentioned. It is sometimes possible to find a relocated web page by typing in the address of the home page for a website in the URL window of your browser.

Orders: please contact Bookpoint Ltd, 130 Milton Park, Abingdon, Oxon OX14 4SB. Telephone: (44) 01235 827720. Fax: (44) 01235 400454. Lines are open 9.00–17.00, Monday to Saturday, with a 24-hour message answering service. Visit our website at www.hoddereducation.co.uk

© Kornel Kossuth 2014

First published in 2014 by
Hodder Education
An Hachette UK Company,
Carmelite House, 50 Victoria Embankment,
London EC4Y 0DZ

Impression number 5 4 3
Year 2018 2017 2016

Typeset in Bembo Std-Regular 12/14 by Datapage (India) Pvt. Ltd.

Printed in England by Hobbs the Printers Ltd, Totton, Hampshire SO40 3WX

A catalogue record for this title is available from the British Library

ISBN 978 1 4718 0414 4

HODDER EDUCATION
www.hoddereducation.co.uk

ISBN 978-1-4718-0414-4

9 781471 804144